GLENCOE LANGUAGE ARTS

Revising with Style

High School

Glencoe McGraw-Hill

New York, New York   Columbus, Ohio   Woodland Hills, California   Peoria, Illinois

To the Teacher

Revising with Style is a blackline master workbook that offers instruction and exercises to help students improve their writing skills. The exercises focus on the process of revision and cover a range of topics, from proofreading and correcting common grammatical errors to combining sentences and reordering them in logical sequences. *Revising with Style* encourages students to think more clearly and to write more effectively.

Glencoe/McGraw-Hill

A Division of The **McGraw·Hill** Companies

Printed in the United States of America.

Send all inquiries to:
Glencoe/McGraw-Hill
8787 Orion Place
Columbus, Ohio 43240

ISBN 0-07-824699-7

2 3 4 5 6 7 8 9 10 045 04 03 02 01

Revising with Style

Contents

SPECIAL TOPICS

Revising with Style

Choosing Effective Details

When you're ready to revise a draft of your writing, ask yourself whether you've expressed yourself in the best possible way. How can adding information and revising your word choice make your writing more powerful, convincing, and interesting to read? If you're not sure how to tackle a revision, the following ideas can give you a place to start.

- If you're writing a **description,** use evocative adjectives and sensory details.

  Delicate violets and fire-orange tiger lilies carpeted the lush ravine.

- If you're writing a **narrative,** use vivid verbs and adverbs that show how the action unfolds.

  I was sleeping peacefully when my little brother marched into my room and slammed the door behind him.

- If you're writing **exposition,** use carefully selected examples, facts, and reasons to support your ideas.

  Some species of gecko can run across ceilings just as easily as they can run across floors. How do these lizards do it? Rows of tiny hairs with thousands of split ends are arranged in a leaflike pattern on the bottoms of their toe pads. The attraction between these hairs and even the smoothest surface enables the gecko to grab and hold on.

- If you're doing **persuasive writing,** use effective evidence and specific words to convince others to support your viewpoint.

  Visit St. Augustine, Florida, the oldest city in the United States. It's a wonderful vacation destination for families because there is something for everyone: sandy beaches, historical sites, interesting shops, and music festivals.

EXERCISE A Incorporate the details listed in parentheses at the end of each sentence, adding or replacing words as needed. Your revision should be more colorful, convincing, and compelling than the original.

Sample   As the bottle began to go out to sea, a wave came and brought it back to the shore. (crashed, drift, enormous, pushed)

Revision   As the bottle began to drift out to sea, an enormous wave crashed and pushed it back to the shore.

1. Throughout the day in the desert, a gecko stayed out of the heat, resting in the shade of a rock. (gravelly, jutting, sweltering)

   _____

   _____

2. The gecko waited for the sun to set and the air to cool before it went out for food. (foraged, patiently)

   _____

   _____

Revising with Style

3. When night fell, the gecko came out from under the rock. (darted, hungry)

_____

_____

4. A grasshopper was the gecko's first meal: the gecko saw the grasshopper near a plant, caught it, and then ate it whole. (cactus, snatched, swallowed, unsuspecting)

_____

_____

5. The gecko didn't stay to enjoy the bug; it sensed snakes and ran away. (nearby, savor, scurried)

_____

_____

EXERCISE B Revise the following paragraphs and rewrite them on the lines provided, adding details and descriptions from your own imagination to make the paragraphs more effective and interesting to read. Feel free to combine sentences and revise the word choice as needed.

The day was too nice to do nothing at all. Janine and Hilary set out to hear a concert in the park. They had made a picnic dinner. They had prepared several different kinds of food. Then they packed everything up and left for the park.

Though they had a lot of things to carry and the trip to the park was long, it was worth it. They knew that their favorite musician would be playing. They arrived with time to spare. They found a good place to sit and waited for the concert.

They were talking and eating when the concert began. The two friends became quiet and listened. They were having so much fun that they could hardly believe the sun was already going down when the concert was over. They would remember this day, the two agreed, and they returned home.

_____

_____

_____

_____

_____

_____

_____

_____

_____

_____

Revising with Style

Saying More with Less

When you revise your writing, look for ways to say more with less. By shortening wordy phrases, you can make your sentences more effective and your writing more concise. Notice the difference between the first sentence below and the two that follow.

Wordy	I wore a coat **for the reason that** I was cold.
Concise	I wore a coat **because** I was cold.
Concise	I wore a coat **since** I was cold.

The phrase *for the reason that* may be familiar to the ear, but the words *because* and *since* work just as well—and in a shorter space. Compare the two columns below and notice how some common but wordy phrases can be sensibly shortened.

Wordy	Concise
as to whether	whether
due to the fact that	because *or* since
during the period that	when
he is someone who	he
in a quick manner	quickly
prior to	before
regardless of the fact that	although *or* even though
subsequent to	after
with regard to	about

You may be tempted to use wordy phrases like the ones shown above when writing formal school reports or business letters. While these phrases may lend a more formal tone, they may also make your writing sound unnatural or inauthentic. Strive to find your own writing voice—without using wordy phrases like these.

EXERCISE Rewrite each of the following sentences, replacing wordy phrases with shorter, more concise terms.

Sample	What do you know concerning the matter of Mary H. Kingsley?
Revision	*What do you know about Mary H. Kingsley?*

1. Born in England in 1862, Kingsley was a person who spent much of her youth caring for her sickly mother and brother.

_____

_____

2. Her father expected her to take care of them owing to the fact that he traveled a great deal.

_____

_____

3. In the little free time she had, however, she would read stories that explorers had written in reference to their adventures in Africa.

_____

_____

_____

4. Subsequent to her parents' death, Kingsley decided to change her life.

_____

_____

5. At the time that she was thirty, she made her first trip to West Africa.

_____

_____

6. Although she was uncertain as to whether she could manage on her own, her trip was a success.

_____

_____

7. Kingsley was someone who felt more at home in West Africa than in England.

_____

_____

8. She lived for a year with the Fang tribe, who accepted her due to the fact that she brought cloth and tobacco to trade for their ivory and rubber.

_____

_____

9. Regardless of the fact that she had no formal education, Kingsley made many scientific discoveries during her trips to West Africa.

_____

_____

_____

Revising with Style

10. Prior to returning to England in 1895, she collected many new and rare species of beetle and fish and made careful ethnological studies of tribal culture.

_____

_____

_____

11. Her travels along the Ogowé River and through jungle to the Rembwé River were all the more remarkable considering the fact that the region had never been mapped.

_____

_____

_____

12. Prior to her, nobody had climbed the northeast face of Mount Cameroon, an ascent of 13,350 feet.

_____

_____

13. When Kingsley fell through a camouflaged animal trap onto twelve-inch spikes, she handled the crisis in a brave manner.

_____

_____

_____

14. The books she wrote with regard to her travels were immediate bestsellers.

_____

_____

15. More than a century following the time that her first book was published, Kingsley continues to be admired by thousands of readers.

_____

_____

_____

Revising with Style

Correcting Commonly Misused Terms I

Be careful when you write not to say one thing when you mean another. Some words and expressions—because they are similar or akin to other words and expressions—are commonly misused. Studying them together can help you use them correctly.

Consider the similar-sounding words *accept* and *except*. Whereas *accept* is a verb that means "to receive" or "to agree to," *except* is usually a preposition that means "but" or "other than." Study the following example:

> Most stores in the United States do not *accept* Canadian money. They refuse all currency *except* U.S. dollars.

A few of the many commonly misused terms are listed below.

a, an *A* and *an* are both articles, but *a* is used before words that begin with either a consonant or a "yew" sound. *An* is used before words that begin with either a vowel or an unsounded *h*.

all ready, already *All ready* means "completely ready." *Already* is an adverb that means "before" or "by this time."

all together, altogether *All together* means "in a group." *Altogether* is an adverb that means "completely" or "on the whole."

between, among *Between* shows the relationship of one person or thing to another. *Among* shows the relationship of more than two persons or things.

could of *Could of* is grammatically incorrect; use *could have* instead.

its, it's *Its* is a pronoun showing possession. *It's* is a contraction meaning "it is."

learn, teach *Learn* means "to gain knowledge." *Teach* means "to instruct, to give knowledge to."

passed, past *Passed* is always the past tense of the verb "to pass." *Past* can be a noun, adjective, preposition, or adverb.

precede, proceed *Precede* means "to go before" or "to come before." *Proceed* means "to continue" or "to move along."

than, then *Than* is usually a conjunction used in comparisons, as in "That stereo costs more than I can afford." *Then* is usually an adverb meaning "at that time," "soon afterward," "for that reason," or "in that case."

EXERCISE Underline the misused word or expression in each of the following sentences. Then write the correct word or expression on the line provided. If a sentence is correct, write *correct*.

Sample _____teach_____ Did your parents <u>learn</u> you how to handle money?

1. _____ In the distant passed, people didn't use money to buy things.

2. _____ Bartering proceeded money.

Revising with Style

Revising with Style

3. _____ What is bartering? It's a direct exchange of goods and services.

4. _____ If you were a sheepherder living under the barter system, you could of gone to a market to exchange sheep for grain.

5. _____ If the sack of grain was worth only half a sheep, than you might have had a problem.

6. _____ Of course, getting the sheep to the market might all ready have been a problem.

7. _____ Money was invented to make a exchange of goods or services easier.

8. _____ If you had to choose among paying for things with sheep or with dollar bills, which would you prefer?

9. _____ You'd want to use the lightest, smallest, most durable form of purchasing power a seller would except.

10. _____ Given that paper money is light, small, and durable, it's altogether understandable why paper money works so well.

Revising with Style

Correcting Commonly Misused Terms II

Many words and expressions are commonly misused. One way to avoid using them incorrectly is to memorize them—and to think before you write.

amount, number While both *amount* and *number* refer to quantity, use *amount* with nouns that cannot be counted; use *number* with nouns that can be counted.

can, may *Can* indicates the ability to do something. *May* indicates the permission to do it. *May* also means "might," as in "I may go to the bank today."

different from, different than *Different from* is preferable to *different than*.

farther, further *Farther* refers to physical distance; *further* refers to degree or time.

irregardless, regardless *Irregardless* is incorrect because it is a double negative: the prefix *ir-* and the suffix *-less* both have negative meanings. Use *regardless* instead.

leave, let *Leave* means "to go away" or "to depart." *Let* means "to allow" or "to permit."

less, fewer *Less* refers to things that cannot be counted; *fewer* usually refers to things that can be counted.

loose, lose *Loose* is an adjective that means "free" or "not fitting tightly." *Lose* is a verb meaning "to have no longer," "to misplace," or "to fail to win."

raise, rise *Raise* is a transitive verb meaning "to cause to move up." *Rise* is an intransitive verb meaning "to get up" or "to move up."

sit, set *Sit* means "to be seated"; *set* means "to put" or "to place."

whose, who's *Whose* is a pronoun showing possession. *Who's* is a contraction of "who is."

EXERCISE Underline the misused word or expression in each of the following sentences. Then write the correct word or expression on the line provided. If a sentence is correct, write *correct*.

Sample _____ Who's _____ Whose going to know if it's real gold or not?

1. _____ Paper bills are much lighter than gold coins, and because they come in larger denominations ($5, $10, and so on), you can carry fewer of them.

2. _____ A farther advantage of paper money is that it is more difficult to counterfeit than gold.

3. _____ It's also easier to control the amount of dollars in circulation if the dollars are made of paper.

4. _____ Now people often use credit cards, which are different than any earlier form of money.

Revising with Style

5. _____ Their money sets in the bank until the credit-card bill is due.

6. _____ People's credit cards could be stolen, yet they wouldn't loose any money if they canceled their cards immediately.

7. _____ A credit-card company will occasionally rise the interest rates that people have to pay.

8. _____ However, people who pay their bills on time avoid paying interest, irregardless of the rate.

9. _____ May you predict how much a hundred dollars will buy fifty years from now?

10. _____ If you put a hundred dollars in the bank now and let it there, it will earn compound interest.

Revising with Style

Using Pronouns Correctly

When you review your writing, check to be sure that each pronoun agrees in person with its antecedent. One common pronoun error is the use of a second-person pronoun (*you*) to refer to a third-person antecedent. To fix such an error, change *you* to an appropriate third-person pronoun as shown in the examples below.

Incorrect	At one time, anyone could find shelter if you looked hard enough.
Correct	At one time, **anyone** could find shelter if **he or she** looked hard enough.
Incorrect	My relatives lived a whole summer in a tent, which you could set up almost anywhere.
Correct	My **relatives** lived a whole summer in a tent, which **they** could set up almost anywhere.

When the antecedent of a pronoun is another pronoun, be sure the two pronouns agree in person. Do not shift from *I* to *you, they* to *you,* or *one* to *you.*

Incorrect	I like it when you can sleep outdoors in warm weather.
Correct	I like it when **I** can sleep outdoors in warm weather.
Incorrect	They set up camp on the ridge, where you can see the horizon.
Correct	**They** set up camp on the ridge, where **they** can see the horizon.
Incorrect	If one enjoys astronomy, you can watch the constellations all night.
Correct	If **one** enjoys astronomy, **one** can watch the constellations all night.

EXERCISE Correct the following sentences, eliminating the inappropriate use of *you* by writing either a third-person pronoun or a suitable noun on the line.

Sample _____*they*_____ Centuries ago, Native Americans lived in the San Francisco Bay area, where you could build various types of houses.

1. _____ The Native Americans made dome-shaped houses out of bulrushes, which you called tule.

2. _____ Adults would build a framework; you would take branches from willow trees and drive them into the ground.

3. _____ Even a small child could help gather the tule, which you would bundle and tie onto the willow framework.

4. _____ The children would help pack down the earthen floor, and then you would put sleeping mats on it.

5. _____ Since people found housing materials growing all around them, you were never homeless for long.

Revising with Style

Using *Only*

When revising your writing, check to be sure that the modifiers are where they belong. If you put a modifier in the wrong place, the meaning of your words may be unclear or you may deliver an unintended message.

An especially tricky modifier is the adverb *only*—a small word that has a big effect on meaning. As a general rule, place *only* immediately before the word or group of words it modifies. Take a look at the sentence below:

A few men in the United States are named **only** Bertram.

This sentence seems to say that a few men in the United States are named just Bertram—they have neither a middle name nor a last name. The writer probably meant to say that there aren't many men in the United States named Bertram. The sentence should be revised as follows:

Only a few men in the United States are named Bertram.

EXERCISE None of the sentences below reflect the writer's intended meaning because the word *only* is in the wrong position. Given the meaning described in parentheses at the end of each sentence, use an arrow to mark the correct position of *only*.

Sample   Most people know the first name of only the painter Raphael.
(Most people don't know his last name was Sanzio.)

1. Some people think that having the right name is the path only to success.
(There is no other path.)

2. There was a time when movie stars and con artists only changed their names. (No one else did.)

3. The model Norma Jean Baker, for example, changed her name to Marilyn Monroe a short while only after signing her first contract with a film studio. (She changed her name not long after signing.)

4. A few people only know that John Wayne was the stage name of Marion Morrison.
(Most people do not know.)

5. John Wayne was not only the actor's stage name; he appeared in his first few films as Duke Morrison. (He had more than one stage name.)

6. Mathilda isn't the name that means only "brave." (Other names also mean "brave.")

7. Graham, however, means only "from the gray house." (No other name means that.)

8. In most states, an application and a birth certificate are only needed to change one's name legally. (One doesn't need anything else to change his or her name legally.)

Revising with Style

Correcting Double Negatives

When you revise your writing, check to be sure that you haven't made the mistake of using a **double negative**—two negative words in the same clause. The clause *I don't have none* contains two negative words—the contraction *don't* and the adjective *none*. If you *don't* have *none*, then you *do* have *some*. To express a negative idea, you should use only one negative word.

In addition to such negative words as *never, no, none,* and *not,* the words *scarcely, hardly,* and *barely* function as negatives and should not be used with other negative words in the same clause.

Read the examples below and notice how some sentences that include double negatives may be revised in more than one way.

Incorrect	He *never* cooks *nothing* exciting for dinner.
Correct	He *never* cooks *anything* exciting for dinner.
Incorrect	We *can't hardly* wait for a change in the menu.
Correct	We *can hardly* wait for a change in the menu.
Correct	We *can't* wait for a change in the menu.
Incorrect	You *haven't* been reading *no* books on how to cook bugs, have you?
Correct	You *haven't* been reading *any* books on how to cook bugs, have you?
Correct	You *haven't* been reading books on how to cook bugs, have you?

EXERCISE Rewrite the following sentences, eliminating the double negative in each. If a sentence is correct, write *correct*.

Sample	Haven't you never tasted a bug?
Revision	Have you never tasted a bug? *or* Haven't you ever tasted a bug?

1. I know people that can't hardly stand the idea of dining on bugs.

   _____

   _____

2. There isn't nothing wrong with eating bugs.

   _____

   _____

3. In some Latin American countries, people don't have no objection to eating the eggs of aquatic insects.

   _____

   _____

Revising with Style

4. It couldn't be no simpler than placing mats underwater for the insects to lay their eggs on.

   _____

   _____

5. Once the eggs are laid, gatherers don't wait none to dry the insects' eggs before making the eggs into cakes.

   _____

   _____

   _____

6. In some African countries, the larvae of honeybees aren't no less popular than their honey.

   _____

   _____

7. If you're in the tropics, you shouldn't get too fond of no dragonflies; they may be ground into a paste and served to you.

   _____

   _____

   _____

8. Can no one in this country see that bugs are an excellent source of protein?

   _____

   _____

9. Somebody had once tried a chocolate-covered grasshopper and hadn't barely noticed the grasshopper.

   _____

   _____

   _____

10. Don't say nothing against bug dishes until you've tried them.

    _____

    _____

Revising with Style

Using Active and Passive Voice

When you're ready to revise a piece of writing, ask yourself whether your words will actively engage your readers' attention and imagination. To ensure that your writing is interesting and exciting to read, check to see whether you've primarily used verbs in the active voice. Remember that an action verb is in the **active voice** when the subject of the sentence performs the action. An action verb is in the **passive voice** when its action is performed on the subject.

Active voice   She blurted out the answer.

Passive voice   The answer was blurted out by her.

Notice how the first sentence is lively and direct, while the second is wordy and dull. You can improve your writing by revising instances where you've used the passive instead of the active voice.

There are times, however, when the passive voice is useful. As a general rule, use the passive voice when you don't know who performed the action, when the performer is unimportant, or when you want to conceal the performer's identity. The sentences below show appropriate uses of the passive voice.

- Animal images **were painted** on the walls of the cave.
  (Who painted them is unknown.)

- Rome **was** not **built** in a day. (Who built it is unimportant.)

- Mistakes **were made.** (The writer doesn't want to identify who made them.)

EXERCISE The sentences below are written in the passive voice. Rewrite each sentence in the active voice; however, when the use of the passive voice is appropriate, write *correct*.

Sample   A quirk of the brain is shared by ten people in a million.

Revision   *Ten people in a million share a quirk of the brain.*

1. Five senses—sight, hearing, smell, taste, and touch—are experienced by all of us.

   _____

   _____

2. For a few people, those five senses are tangled together.

   _____

   _____

3. Shapes are heard by some of them.

   _____

   _____

Revising with Style

4. Colors are tasted by others.

_____

_____

5. This quirk of the brain is perceived differently by different people.

_____

_____

6. It is called *synesthesia.*

_____

_____

7. "Sensing together" is meant by *synesthesia,* a combination of the Greek words *syn* (together) and *aisthesis* (sensation).

_____

_____

8. In people with synesthesia, one sense is triggered by another.

_____

_____

9. Synesthesia has been lived with by many creative people.

_____

_____

10. The letters of the alphabet were seen in colors by writer Vladimir Nabokov.

_____

_____

11. The letter *k,* for example, was perceived by him as huckleberry blue.

_____

_____

12. Colors were associated with musical tones by the composer Aleksandr Scriabin.

_____

_____

Revising with Style

13. An A-major chord was heard by him as green.

_____

_____

14. Flavors were perceived as shapes by one person.

_____

_____

15. A bland chicken was once described by this person as not having "enough points."

_____

_____

16. Baked beans were tasted by another person at the sound of the word *Francis*.

_____

_____

17. The existence of synesthesia has been known for over two hundred years.

_____

_____

18. It has been figured out by scientists only in the last few decades, however.

_____

_____

19. It was concluded by a leading researcher that everyone's brain is capable of synesthesia.

_____

_____

20. Even so, conscious awareness of it is reached by only a few people.

_____

_____

Revising with Style

Varying Sentence Openers

Evaluate the sentence structures in any piece of published writing—from novels to news articles—and you're sure to notice one thing: sentence variety is the key to writing that flows gracefully from one sentence to the next. If you structure all the sentences in a paragraph the same way—subject followed by verb followed by direct object, for example—your paragraph will sound boring and repetitive. Altering the way in which your own sentences begin is one way to introduce sentence variety and improve the flow of your writing. Some of the ways to vary your sentence openers are listed below.

- **Start with adjectives or adverbs.**

  Deep green, shiny, and clear, the emerald sparkled in the jeweler's case. (adjectives)

  Loudly and insistently, my mother called me to dinner. (adverbs)

- **Start with a prepositional phrase.**

  During rush hour, I avoid the freeway.

- **Start with a participle or participial phrase.**

  Shouting his dog's name, Ross headed for the park. (present participial phrase)

  Cooked to perfection, my father's meal beckoned us to eat. (past participial phrase)

- **Start with an absolute phrase.**

  All things considered, it was a good day.

You can also use more than one of these options, as in the following example:

  Quickly, without fanfare, Eliot handed out the gifts. (adverb + prepositional phrase)

EXERCISE Each item below begins with a sentence model from literature that has an interesting sentence opener. Combine the sentences that follow into a single sentence that matches the structure of the literature model. You may omit words or change their forms as you combine sentence parts.

Sample   Conscience-stricken, Leo rose and brewed the tea.   Bernard Malamud, "The Magic Barrel"

- Beth was satisfied.
- Beth pushed her chair back from the dinner table and excused herself.

Revision   Satisfied, Beth pushed her chair back from the dinner table and excused herself.

1. Fumbling with both hands, he once more stuck the knife into the sheath.   Isak Dinesen, "The Ring"

- The members of the band sounded as good as ever.
- They were playing together for the first time in years.

_____

_____

Revising with Style

2. In his room, he plays his guitar. John Updike, "Son"
    - Nate paints watercolors.
    - He paints them in his mother's studio.

    _____

    _____

3. Creaking, jerking, jostling, gasping, the train filled the station. Nadine Gordimer, "The Train from Rhodesia"
    - The tractor pushed against the heavy log.
    - The tractor was grinding, growling, whistling, and hiccuping.

    _____

    _____

4. Eyes narrowing, he thought for a few moments about what to do.
    Jack Finney, "Contents of the Dead Man's Pocket"
    - The yacht headed out to open sea.
    - Sails were billowing.

    _____

    _____

5. Gaunt, bruised, and shaken, he stumbled back to his village. Lame Deer, "The Vision Quest"
    - The dog was well-fed, energetic, and happy.
    - The dog headed outside to play.

    _____

    _____

6. Frightened, everyone in the village fled into the canes. Paule Marshall, "To Da-duh, in Memoriam"
    - The bull was angered.
    - The bull charged the matador.

    _____

    _____

7. The staircase window having been boarded up, no light came down into the hall.
    Elizabeth Bowen, "The Demon Lover"
    - The bicycle tire had been punctured.
    - Jasmine had to walk the bicycle home.

    _____

    _____

Revising with Style

8. Patient, cold, and callous, our hands wrapped in socks, we waited to snowball the cats.

   Dylan Thomas, "A Child's Christmas in Wales"

   • The producer accepted the Oscar for best picture.
   • She was wide-eyed, joyful, and proud.
   • Her head was lifted high.

   _____

   _____

9. Slowly, taking my time, I began the final ascent.

   Arthur C. Clarke, "The Sentinel"

   • Leo ran toward the goal line.
   • He ran swiftly.
   • He was holding the football firmly in his arms.

   _____

   _____

10. For the first time since my arrival, I was very nearly home.

    Maya Angelou, *All God's Children Need Traveling Shoes*

    • Polly could run a five-minute mile.
    • She had been able to run a five-minute mile for more than a month.

    _____

    _____

Revising with Style

Splitting Subject and Verb I

By using a word or phrase to split the subject and verb of a sentence, you can add descriptive detail or build suspense for the reader. Some common ways and examples of splitting the subject and the verb are listed below.

- **Add adjectives.**

  The town barber, *quiet and dignified,* was waiting for the next customer.

- **Add a prepositional phrase.**

  The hotel attendant, *with one swift motion,* hoisted five bags of luggage.

- **Add an appositive or appositive phrase.**

  Dr. Tompkins, *the speaker for the evening,* thanked the audience for their questions.

- **Add a participle or participial phrase.**

  The panther at the zoo, *pacing back and forth in its cage,* seemed ready to pounce.

  The Empire State Building, *completed in 1931,* was once the tallest building on Earth.

EXERCISE Each item below begins with a sentence model taken from literature. Unscramble the jumbled phrases that follow to create a new sentence that matches the structure of the literature model. Add commas to the beginning and end of each phrase splitting a subject and verb.

Sample   Mr. DePalma, to our complete shock, was crying.   Judith Ortiz Cofer, "American History"

- laughed at every joke in the movie
- in the seat beside him
- his daughter

Revision   *His daughter, in the seat beside him, laughed at every joke in the movie.*

1. That summer, the summer of 1918, was blighted.   James Hurst, "The Scarlet Ibis"

- a tenant on the fifth floor
- plays the piano every night
- one tenant

_____

_____

2. The shopman, in some dim cavern of his mind, may have dared to think so too.   Katherine Mansfield, "A Cup of Tea"

- was closing in on a world record
- the Olympic swimmer
- with every stroke and every kick

_____

_____

Revising with Style

3. The scientific weeds, seen from close up, looked straggly and gnarled.

Anne Tyler, "With All Flags Flying"

- tasted better than she remembered
- baked entirely from scratch
- her grandmother's pie

_____

_____

4. The forests, somber and dull, stood motionless and silent on each side of the broad stream.

Joseph Conrad, "The Lagoon"

- the basketball fans
- packed into the arena to cheer on their team
- loud and lively

_____

_____

5. Her other arm, swinging loose, was very white in the sun.

Doris Lessing, "Through the Tunnel"

- meeting in secret
- a group of Hollywood actors
- formed the Screen Actors Guild in 1933

_____

_____

6. The former tenant of our house, a priest, had died in the back drawing room.

James Joyce, "Araby"

- was virtually eradicated through vaccinations
- a deadly virus
- smallpox

_____

_____

7. The Monster, at the first motion, lunged forward with a terrible scream.

Ray Bradbury, "A Sound of Thunder"

- in less than ten minutes
- had flooded the entire street
- the broken water main

_____

_____

Revising with Style

8. The liquid avalanche, known as a lahar, was soon hurtling down the steep slopes at speeds of up to 30 m.p.h.

George Russell, "Colombia's Mortal Agony"

- paralyzed in his legs since the age of four
- Itzhak Perlman
- is considered to be one of the world's premier violinists

_____

_____

9. E. J. Kenney, the marshal dispatched to arrest Susan B. Anthony, was not at all happy with his assignment.

Margaret Truman, "The United States vs. Susan B. Anthony"

- John Logie Baird
- was the first person to televise moving objects
- a pioneer in television technology

_____

_____

10. The piano, having gone away to be stored, had left what looked like claw marks on its part of the parquet.

Elizabeth Bowen, "The Demon Lover"

- was still perplexed
- the detective
- having rummaged the crime scene for clues

_____

_____

Revising with Style · LESSON 11

Splitting Subject and Verb II

During the revision process, you may wish to create sentence variety by splitting the subject and verb with a word or phrase. Doing so, however, should not affect the subject-verb agreement. If the subject is singular, use a singular verb. If the subject is plural, use a plural verb.

Notice in the following examples that the subject and verb, no matter how far apart they are, always agree.

- The **construction** of a bridge, requiring hundreds of people and millions of dollars, **takes** years of planning.

- **Joseph B. Strauss,** a designer of nearly four hundred bridges, **is** known today for having built the Golden Gate Bridge.

EXERCISE A For each sentence below, rewrite the underlined verb so that it agrees with its subject. If the verb is correct, write *correct*.

Sample _____ visit _____ Nearly nine million people, from all over the world, visits the Golden Gate Bridge each year.

1. _____ The Golden Gate Bridge, linking San Francisco and Marin counties, were completed in 1937.

2. _____ The impressive look of this suspension bridge, bright orange in color and art deco in style, was the idea of consulting architects Irving and Gertrude Morrow.

3. _____ The bright orange, despite the U.S. Navy's preference for black with yellow stripes, were meant to blend with the natural setting.

4. _____ Workers, fighting erosion from the salty air, repaints the bridge almost continuously.

5. _____ Their effort, though unnoticed by most passersby, keep the steel portion of the bridge from rusting away.

EXERCISE B For each numbered item below, combine the sentences so that a phrase splits the subject and verb of the combined sentence. Make sure that the subject and verb agree.

1. The bridge's two main towers rise 746 feet above water.

   The towers are made of structural steel.

   _____

   _____

   _____

Revising with Style

2. New lamps make the towers appear taller at night.

The new lamps were installed after the fiftieth anniversary of the bridge.

_____

_____

_____

3. The bridge's main span measures 4,200 feet.

A bridge's main span is the distance between its two main towers.

_____

_____

_____

4. This span was the longest in the world.

It was the longest for almost thirty years.

_____

_____

_____

5. The Akashi-Kaikyo Bridge in Japan is now the world's longest suspension bridge.

The Akashi-Kaikyo Bridge in Japan has a main span of 6,532 feet.

_____

_____

_____

Revising with Style

Varying Sentence Closers

You can improve the pacing of your writing, add variety, and heighten the reader's interest by varying your sentence closers. Below are a few common ways to end a sentence.

- **End a sentence with adjectives or adverbs.**

  In the driveway was our new car, *clean and sporty red.* (adjectives)

  The baby began to take its first steps, *slowly, unsteadily.* (adverbs)

- **End a sentence with a prepositional phrase.**

  Reynaldo was in no shape to get up, *not with his aches and fever.*

- **End a sentence with an appositive or appositive phrase.**

  The crowd was awed by her performance, *a real show-stopper.*

- **End a sentence with an absolute phrase.**

  The lion basked in the African sun, *its tail swishing back and forth.*

- **End a sentence with a participle or participial phrase.**

  The children ran alongside the train, *cheering.* (present participle)

  We laughed at our faces, *pulled and stretched impossibly in the fun-house mirror.* (past participial phrase)

EXERCISE A Each item below begins with a sentence model taken from literature. Combine the sentences that follow into a single sentence that matches the structure of the literature model. You may omit or add words or change word forms as necessary.

Sample He stood up against the wall of the drugstore, smoking.

James Thurber, "The Secret Life of Walter Mitty"

- Ellen sat in the doctor's office.
- She was fidgeting.

Revision Ellen sat in the doctor's office, fidgeting.

1. She then gave me the pillow, my mother's pillow. Edwidge Dandicat, "Nineteen Thirty-Seven"

   - We drove over a hundred miles to the cabin.
   - The cabin was our home for the summer.

   _____

   _____

2. Salzman listened in embarrassed surprise, sensing a sort of apology. Bernard Malamud, "The Magic Barrel"

   - My uncle laughed at his own jokes.
   - He was ruining the punch lines.

   _____

   _____

Revising with Style

3. Over the next year I practiced like this, dutifully in my own way.   Amy Tan, "Two Kinds"

- Celia took charge of the situation.
- She took charge decisively but not offensively.

_____

_____

4. An uninhabited house of two stories stood at the blind end, detached from its neighbors in a square ground.   James Joyce, "Araby"

- The window washers' scaffold hung near the top of the skyscraper.
- The scaffold was steadied by nothing more than a few guy wires.

_____

_____

_____

5. It was a hot day, with all the windows and doors open in case a breeze should come.   James Hurst, "The Scarlet Ibis"

- Dad came inside from the bitter cold.
- Icicles were hanging from his moustache and eyebrows.

_____

_____

EXERCISE B Combine the sentences in each item below, using one of the types of sentence closers from the bulleted list. Omit words or change word forms as needed.

1. The defendant stared nervously at the jurors. The defendant was anxious to know their verdict.

_____

_____

2. The Great Balanzini held his arms out and stepped confidently onto the tightrope. He had a blindfold wrapped snugly around his head.

_____

_____

_____

3. The creek floods each May. May is a worrisome month for nearby homeowners.

_____

_____

Revising with Style

4. She examined each egg. She was checking for cracks.

_____

_____

5 Huge cranes moved all about the construction site. They were hauling girders and stacks of bricks.

_____

_____

6. I can't stop thinking about that movie. It was romantic yet hilarious.

_____

_____

7. The waiter hurried to our table. Our pizza was held high above his head.

_____

_____

8. The stream winds for miles through the woods. It ends suddenly in a two-hundred-foot waterfall.

_____

_____

Revising with Style

Adding Clauses

To add variety and detail to your writing, add clauses to your sentences. A **clause** is a group of words that has a subject and a predicate and is used as part of a sentence. A clause that can stand alone as a sentence is called a **main clause.** A clause that cannot stand alone is called a **subordinate clause.** For stylistic effect, you can sometimes add a subordinate clause at various points in a sentence. Study the following examples:

- Today, **because I didn't feel well,** I couldn't go to school.

- My best friend, Monica, **because she didn't feel well,** couldn't go to school either.

- Our teachers must have been curious, **because neither of us has missed a single class before today.**

The groups of words in bold are all subordinate clauses. Notice that these subordinate clauses, while relevant, are not needed to make the meaning of the sentences clear. That is, these subordinate clauses are **nonessential.** When adding a nonessential clause to a sentence, you need to set the clause off with commas.

EXERCISE Each item below begins with a sentence model from literature that has a subordinate clause. Rearrange the bulleted sentence parts to create a new sentence that matches the structure of the literature model. Add commas where necessary.

Sample   Then, as he stepped forward, his foot sank into the ooze.

Richard Connell, "The Most Dangerous Game"

- scientists may find cures for many inherited diseases
- soon
- if gene therapy continues to enjoy success

Revision   Soon, if gene therapy continues to enjoy success, scientists may find cures for many inherited diseases.

1. That spring, when I discovered the lone horned toad near the back of the lot, had been rough on my family.

Gerald Haslam, "The Horned Toad"

- Jackie Robinson
- became the first African American to play major-league baseball
- who joined the Brooklyn Dodgers in 1947

_____

_____

2. The skies, which dawned a clear, blazing blue, have grayed.

Jane Ellen Stevens, "Exploring Antarctic Ice"

- entered World War I as an ambulance driver for the Red Cross
- Ernest Hemingway
- who was rejected for military service several times

_____

_____

Revising with Style

3. After that their manner changed a little toward me, although I was their friend against outsiders.

Ernest Hemingway, "In Another Country"

- even though the number of hours spent surfing the Web has also risen
- the number of books sold each year has risen
- since 1991

_____

_____

4. She wore her coarse, straight hair, which was slightly streaked with gray, in a long braided rope across the top of her head.

Maya Angelou, "Living Well. Living Good."

- which is spoken in both Portugal and Brazil
- Fernando speaks Portuguese
- with the distinctive accent of a Brazilian

_____

_____

5. Nevertheless, as I made the raft, the tears ran out of my eyes.

Stephen Vincent Benét, "By the Waters of Babylon"

- you should wear supportive shoes
- when you jog
- needless to say

_____

_____

6. Once a boy, whose name was Richard, drowned in the river.

James Baldwin, "The Rockpile"

- which use automated photo technology
- new traffic control systems
- may help to discourage drivers from running red lights

_____

_____

Inverting Sentence Order I

In most sentences, the subject precedes the verb. In **inverted sentences,** the verb precedes the subject. To create sentence variety, you can sometimes invert the subject and verb and move a part of the predicate to the beginning of the sentence. In the following examples, notice that the verb precedes the subject, giving more prominence to other parts of speech at the beginning of the sentence.

Beautiful was the landscape. (adjective)
In silence is found peace. (prepositional phrase)
Flying high above us was the majestic bald eagle. (participial phrase)

In questions, one of three kinds of words usually begins a sentence: a verb, a helping verb, or a question word, such as *who, what, where, when, why,* or *how.* When a question begins with a verb or a helping verb, sentence order is always inverted. But when it begins with a question word, sentence order may not be inverted.

Verb   **Is** it time for lunch yet?
Helping verb   **Did** you hear that?
Question word   **Who** wants salad?

EXERCISE Each item below begins with a sentence model taken from literature. Rewrite the sentence that follows to create a new sentence that matches the structure of the literature model.

Sample Farther down the street was Ping Yuen Fish Market.   Amy Tan, "Rules of the Game"

Three varieties of tomato grew in her garden.

Revision In her garden grew three varieties of tomato.

1. On went her old brown jacket; on went her old brown hat.   O. Henry, "The Gift of the Magi"

The streamers came down; the signs came down.

_____

_____

2. Only in the Eighth Ward did the males weaken.   Margaret Truman, "The United States vs. Susan B. Anthony"

One could get in only with an officially stamped ticket.

_____

_____

3. In the middle of the land was the great Sky Tree.   Joseph Bruchac, "The Sky Tree"

A tiny hosta plant grew at the edge of the clearing.

_____

_____

Revising with Style

4. Sad were the lights in the houses opposite.   Katherine Mansfield, "A Cup of Tea"

The children in the yard next door are happy.

_____

_____

5. Directly opposite him, on the other side of the enclosed space, were two doors, exactly alike
and side by side.   Frank R. Stockton, "The Lady, or the Tiger?"

The opera stars stood onstage, in front of the curtain, smiling and bowing deeply before
the crowd.

_____

_____

_____

6. When he telephoned her brother Donnie, was he hoping for her to answer?
                    Anne Tyler, "With All Flags Flying"

She was expecting him to laugh when she made fun of him.

_____

_____

7. In the front yard was a huge oak tree that Luis remembered having climbed during the funeral to
get away from people.   Judith Ortiz Cofer, "Catch the Moon"

A small bronze statue that Maria recalled having studied one evening to inspire her own
art was at the city park.

_____

_____

_____

8. Also lurking around Pius's unpretentious mud hut were newspaper reporters.
                    Barbara Kimenye, "The Winner"

The new puppy was not yet settling into our comfortable little house.

_____

_____

9. Isn't that the funniest thing you have ever heard?   V. S. Naipaul, "B. Wordsworth"

This isn't the best peach she has ever tasted.

_____

_____

Revising with Style

Revising with Style

10. On my desk lay the lance points of ice age hunters and the heavy leg bone of a fossil bison.

Loren Eisley, "The Angry Winter"

Her two grandparents and her four-year-old brother stood alongside her.

_____

_____

11. Out came the servants from the kitchen.

Doris Lessing, "A Mild Attack of Locusts"

The lights went on in every room of the house.

_____

_____

12. Many and long were the conversations between Lord Byron and Shelley, to which I was a devout but nearly silent listener.

Mary Shelley, *Frankenstein*

The path to the base camp, where one could find a cot and a warm meal, was steep and slippery.

_____

_____

_____

Revising with Style

Inverting Sentence Order II

When you revise your writing, it's important that you check to be sure that your subjects and verbs agree. This can be tricky when the word order is inverted and the subject follows the verb. Be careful that you don't mistake another word for the subject. For example, if you identify the object of a preposition or the subject of a subordinate clause as the subject, you may use a verb that does not agree in number with the true subject. Study the following example.

Through the winding streets **rides** Eric on his bike.

The subject of the sentence is *Eric,* not *streets* (the object of the preposition *through*). Therefore, the verb *rides* is singular, agreeing in number with its subject.

EXERCISE For each sentence below, write in the space provided the correct form of the underlined verb or helping verb. If the verb is correct, write *C.*

Sample _____is_____ Excited and relieved <u>are</u> Jenny when she moves into her first apartment.

1. _____ In her hands <u>are</u> the key to her own front door.

2. _____ Over there <u>is</u> her comfortable chair and her fireplace.

3. _____ Throughout the rooms <u>wafts</u> the delicious odor of apple pie.

4. _____ Very different from her family home <u>is</u> the surroundings of her own place.

5. _____ What <u>is</u> her sisters and brothers doing right now?

6. _____ Much as she loves them, such noise <u>does</u> they create!

7. _____ So relaxed <u>is</u> Jenny that it takes her several days to remember that she hasn't paid her rent yet.

8. _____ Where <u>is</u> her rent check and stamps?

9. _____ Under the newspapers and magazines <u>lurk</u> the rent check.

10. _____ Only after searching for hours <u>do</u> she find it.

Revising with Style   LESSON 16

Revising for Parallelism I

The goal of writing is to communicate ideas, and sentence structure is the framework
used to support those ideas. When you write a properly constructed sentence, chances
are your readers won't even notice how it has been put together. Improperly
constructed sentences, however, are awkward, and this awkwardness interferes with
your reader's ability to give full attention to your message.

   When you find an awkward sentence in your writing, check to see whether you
need to revise for parallelism. In a sentence with **parallel construction,** the same
grammatical form is used for a series of words, phrases, or clauses. For example, if a
prepositional phrase is used for the first idea, prepositional phrases should be used for
the related ideas that follow. If a gerund or a participle is used for the first, gerunds or
participles should be used for the others.

Not parallel	**To write** and **communicating** are not necessarily the same thing.
Parallel	**To write** and **to communicate** are not necessarily the same thing.
Parallel	**Writing** and **communicating** are not necessarily the same thing.

If an article (*a, an,* or *the*) or a preposition (such as *for, at,* or *in*) applies to all the items
in the series, it should appear before only the first item or before every item.

Not parallel	Revising is important **for** essays, **for** stories, and other formal writing.
Parallel	Revising is important **for** essays, stories, and other formal writing.
Parallel	Revising is important **for** essays, **for** stories, and **for** other formal writing.

This rule should also be applied to pronouns, such as *who* and *that,* and to helping
verbs, such as *am, is, have, had, can, could, will,* and *would.*

Not parallel	I **had researched** the topic, **made** an outline, and **had written** a draft.
Parallel	I **had researched** the topic, **made** an outline, and **written** a draft.
Parallel	I **had researched** the topic, **had made** an outline, and **had written** a draft.

EXERCISE Revise each sentence to make its structure parallel. If necessary, you may omit
words, rearrange their order, or change their forms.

Sample   The play I saw was clever, with romance, and it had lots of emotion.

Revision   *The play I saw was clever, romantic, and emotional.*

1. There are many types of plays, including drama, tragedy, and comical.

   _____

   _____

2. Plays may be presented in theaters, open-air spaces, empty stores, or in school auditoriums.

   _____

   _____

Name _____   Date _____

Revising with Style

3. A play should be exciting, entertaining, and a meaningful experience for the audience.

_____

_____

4. Reading a script is easy, but to make a script into a production is challenging.

_____

_____

5. Even a play with only one act and having two characters requires much cooperative effort.

_____

_____

6. A director's work consists of analyzing the play, the casting of the roles, work with technicians, and supervision of the entire production.

_____

_____

7. Actors must understand their roles, determine their characters' feelings and motivations, and must decide how to move and speak.

_____

_____

8. Besides actors, the artists involved with a play include a scenic designer, lighting designer, and a costume designer.

_____

_____

9. The lighting designer arranges multicolored lights to illuminate a scene and supporting its mood.

_____

_____

10. When various productions of the same play are compared, one may notice vast differences in lighting, scenery, and in sound effects.

_____

_____

Revising with Style

Revising for Parallelism II

To revise for parallelism, make sure that the same grammatical form is used for a series of words, phrases, or clauses. In the first example sentence below, the parts of the series following the word *because* are not parallel. The first two parts, *it was clumsy* and *it was too long* are both clauses. The third part, *due to its lack of clarity,* is a phrase. The sentence has been revised in three ways. Which revision do you prefer?

Not parallel	I rewrote the sentence because it was clumsy, it was too long, and due to its lack of clarity.
Parallel	I rewrote the sentence because **it was clumsy, it was too long,** and **it lacked clarity.**
Parallel	I rewrote the sentence because of **its clumsiness, its length,** and **its lack of clarity.**
Parallel	I rewrote the sentence because it was **clumsy, long,** and **unclear.**

Also check for parallelism in sentences that contain pairs of correlative conjunctions, such as *both . . . and, not only . . . but also, either . . . or, neither . . . nor,* or *whether . . . or.* The sentence structure after the second correlative conjunction should be exactly parallel in form to the structure after the first correlative conjunction.

Not parallel	Both the ideas in a paper and presenting them are important.
Parallel	Both **the ideas** in a paper and **their presentation** are important.
Parallel	Both **the ideas** in a paper and **the presentation of them** are important.

EXERCISE Revise each sentence to make its structure parallel. If necessary, you may omit words, rearrange their order, or change their forms. If a sentence is correct, write *correct.*

Sample The theater had good acoustics, with modern lighting, and its fire exits were well marked.

Revision *The theater had good acoustics, modern lighting, and well-marked fire exits.*

1. Audiences won't enjoy a play that is boring, long, or that confuses them.

_____

_____

2. A successful director not only recognizes a good script but also he can bring that script to life.

_____

_____

3. Actors are, of course, critical to a play's effectiveness and whether it is a success.

_____

_____

Revising with Style

4. Good actors take care both in speaking their lines well and in their use of even the smallest gestures.

_____

_____

5. A makeup artist can change an actor's appearance through the application of color and shadows or by using devices such as beards, scars, and wigs.

_____

_____

6. Understanding emotions and portraying them effectively are critical to actors.

_____

_____

7. A costume designer researches the time period in which the drama is set, designs costumes for the actors that are true to the period, and then the designer is supervising the manufacture of the clothing.

_____

_____

_____

8. The designer's work must both reflect and it must be supportive of the action, time period, mood, and theme of the play.

_____

_____

9. Drama critics should be people who are familiar with many types of plays and having a well-developed artistic taste.

_____

_____

10. Drama critics must be forming their own opinions about a play but also be mindful of the message that the director, cast, and designers are trying to convey.

_____

_____

Revising with Style

Combining Sentences I

Add variety and complexity to your writing by combining strings of simplistic sentences and omitting repeated words. Study the suggestions and examples below.

- **Use a conjunction to join two predicates that share a common subject.**
  a. Prehistoric artists painted with nothing but earth and saliva.
  b. They created images full of life. **[yet]**
  *Prehistoric artists painted with nothing but earth and saliva **yet** created images full of life.*

- **Omit repeated words, using commas to separate words or phrases in a series.** (Notice that the verb form must change to agree with the compound subject.)
  a. Barb is studying cave paintings.
  b. Tim is studying cave paintings.
  c. Maggie is studying cave paintings. **[, and]**
  ***Barb, Tim, and Maggie** are studying cave paintings.*

- **Add modifiers.**
  a. The artist painted a picture.
  b. The artist was young.
  c. The picture was colorful.
  *The **young** artist painted a **colorful** picture.*

- **Change adjectives to adverbs.**
  a. She drew a flower.
  b. She was careful as she drew it. **[-ly]**
  *She **carefully** drew a flower.*

- **Use appositives.**
  a. The paintings are of animals. **[:]**
  b. Some of the animals are bison.
  c. Some of the animals are deer.
  d. Some of the animals are horses. **[, and]**
  *The paintings are of animals: **bison, deer, and horses.***

EXERCISE Combine each cluster of sentences into a single sentence. For the first three clusters, use the clues provided—underlined words and phrases and bracketed words, word parts, and punctuation marks—to help you combine the sentences.

Sample   a. It seems humans have always had impulses.
             b. The impulses are artistic.

Revision   It seems humans have always had artistic impulses.

1. a. The oldest known paintings were created more than thirty thousand years ago.
    b. They have survived undamaged. **[yet]**

_____

_____

Revising with Style

2. a. People living many millennia ago carved objects.
   b. Those people painted images.
   c. Those people built shelters. **[, and]**

_____

_____

3. a. Some animals in cave art have horns.
   b. The horns are exaggerated.
   c. The horns are grotesque. **[-ly]**

_____

_____

4. a. To study prehistoric cultures, anthropologists use several clues.
   b. They use art.
   c. They use fossils.
   d. They use pollens.

_____

_____

5. a. Prehistoric cave paintings were discovered at Lascaux, France.
   b. These prehistoric cave paintings are the best-known ones.
   c. They were discovered more than fifty years ago.

_____

_____

6. a. Other cave paintings have been found.
   b. There are some at Altamira, Spain.
   c. There are some at Vallon-Pont-d'Arc, France.
   d. There are some at Pêche-Merle, France.

_____

_____

7. a. The artists often worked far at the back of cave chambers.
   b. The cave chambers were tiny.
   c. The cave chambers were dimly lit.

_____

_____

Revising with Style

8. a. Lamps have been found in some caves.
   b. The lamps are small.
   c. The lamps are made of stone.

_____

_____

9. a. Michel Lorblanchet is an artist.
   b. He is talented at his art.
   c. He is also a cave archaeologist.

_____

_____

10. a. Lorblanchet has figured out prehistoric artists' techniques.
   b. He has re-created their actual experience.
   c. He has reproduced the Pêche-Merle paintings of horses.

_____

_____

Revising with Style

Combining Sentences II

When revising your writing, look for ways to vary the length and structure of your sentences. One effective way to do this is to combine sentences that are repetitive or simplistic. You can combine such sentences by deleting repeated words, adding connecting words, or changing the form of words. Study the techniques below.

- **Use a coordinating conjunction (*and, but, for, or, nor, so,* or *yet*) to combine clauses.**
  a. Gargoyles can be ugly creatures.
  b. Few people are frightened by them. [**, but**]
  *Gargoyles can be ugly creatures, **but** few people are frightened by them.*

- **Add correlative conjunctions (*either . . . or; not only . . . but also; both . . . and*).**
  a. It's because they're made out of stone.
  b. It's because they're so ugly they're cute. [**either . . . or**]
  *It's **either** because they're made out of stone **or** because they're so ugly they're cute.*

- **Link main clauses with conjunctive adverbs (such as *also, however, moreover, nevertheless, still, therefore*). Use a semicolon before a conjunctive adverb that joins two sentences and use a comma after it.**
  a. Gargoyles are architectural ornaments.
  b. They're functional. [**moreover**]
  *Gargoyles are architectural ornaments**; moreover,** they're functional.*

- **Use possessive nouns or pronouns.**
  a. We looked at a book about gargoyles.
  b. The book belongs to Maria. [**'s**]
  *We looked at **Maria's** book about gargoyles.*

EXERCISE Combine each sentence pair into a single sentence. Where indicated, use the bracketed words, word parts, and punctuation marks in your combined sentences.

Sample   a. Gargoyles are ornate spouts.
            b. They project from the cornices of a building. [**, and**]

Revision   *Gargoyles are ornate spouts, and they project from the cornices of a building.*

1. a. Gargoyles funnel rainwater away from the building.
    b. They watch over passersby. [**not only . . . but also**]

    _____

    _____

2. a. This gargoyle is carved to look like a head.
    b. The head resembles that of a lion. [**'s**]

    _____

    _____

Revising with Style

3. a. Gargoyles must have been popular during the rise of Gothic architecture.
   b. They can be seen on many large buildings over five hundred years old. [, for]

   _____

   _____

4. a. Most people think of gargoyles as creatures from medieval cathedrals.
   b. They are popular to this day. [still]

   _____

   _____

5. a. Modern stone carvers have captured the old gargoyle styles.
   b. They've added some contemporary designs. [not only . . . but also]

   _____

   _____

6. a. Stone carvers worked on the National Cathedral in Washington, D.C., for more than forty years.
   b. They carved only 112 gargoyles. [, yet]

   _____

   _____

7. a. Visitors to the National Cathedral can see a menacing face.
   b. It is the face of Darth Vader. ['s]

   _____

   _____

8. a. They can also see a stone lawyer, complete with briefcase, and a gargoyle in a gas mask.
   b. They know they're not looking at a medieval building. [, so]

   _____

   _____

Revising with Style

Combining Sentences III

When writing to inform, keep in mind that not every piece of information requires its own sentence. To say more in a shorter space, take a phrase from one sentence and add it to another. A **phrase** is a group of related words that does not have a subject and a predicate and that functions in a sentence as a single part of speech. See below for ways to combine sentences by using various kinds of phrases as either adjectives or adverbs.

- **Use prepositional phrases as adjectives.**
  a. The Renaissance was an era.
  b. It was an era of great artistic and intellectual activity.
  *The Renaissance was an era **of great artistic and intellectual activity.***

- **Use participial phrases as adjectives.**
  a. The Renaissance saw discoveries, commercial growth, and a return among scholars to classical ideas and values.
  b. The Renaissance began in the fourteenth century. **[-ing]**
  ***Beginning in the fourteenth century,** the Renaissance saw discoveries, commercial growth, and a return among scholars to classical ideas and values.*

- **Use infinitive phrases as adjectives.**
  a. Many thinkers of the day revered an artist's struggle.
  b. An artist's struggle was about creating. **[to]**
  *Many thinkers of the day revered an artist's struggle **to create.***

- **Use prepositional phrases as adverbs.**
  a. Some of the best painters in history lived and worked in Italy.
  b. They lived there during the fifteenth and sixteenth centuries.
  *Some of the best painters in history lived and worked in Italy **during the fifteenth and sixteenth centuries.***

- **Use infinitive phrases as adverbs.**
  a. Emperors and popes would commission these artists.
  b. The commissions were for adorning palaces, churches, and tombs with their work. **[to]**
  *Emperors and popes would commission these artists **to adorn palaces, churches, and tombs with their work.***

EXERCISE Combine each cluster of sentences so that the new information (underlined) is embedded as an adjective or adverb phrase in sentence *a*. Where indicated, use the bracketed words and word parts in your combined sentences. Add commas where necessary.

Sample   a. Leonardo da Vinci is known throughout the world.
               b. He is known for his painting.

Revision   Leonardo da Vinci is known throughout the world for his painting.

Revising with Style

1. a. Leonardo was born.
   b. He was born in a village called Vinci.
   c. He was born in 1452.

   _____

   _____

2. a. He had a talent.
   b. His talent was for painting colorful, expressive pictures.

   _____

   _____

3. a. Leonardo developed his talent.
   b. He was apprenticed to the artist Verrocchio.
   c. He was apprenticed after moving to Florence at the age of twelve or thirteen.

   _____

   _____

4. a. He set up his own shop.
   b. He set it up after close to twelve years of apprenticeship.

   _____

   _____

5. a. He then made a decision.
   b. His decision was to move to Milan.
   c. He would move to Milan to work for the duke Lodovico Sforza.

   _____

   _____

6. a. Sforza gave Leonardo a commission.
   b. Sforza admired Leonardo's talent. [-ing]
   c. The commission was for painting *The Last Supper*. [to]

   _____

   _____

7. a. Leonardo's *Mona Lisa* quickly became famous.
   b. His *Mona Lisa* was painted after his return to Florence years later.
   c. His *Mona Lisa* became famous for the subject's mysterious expression.

   _____

   _____

Revising with Style

8. a. Leonardo used a painting technique.
   b. The technique was of contrasting light and shadow.
   c. The technique is called *chiaroscuro*.

   _____

   _____

9. a. He also covered his paintings with tinted varnish.
   b. He covered his paintings with varnish to give them a hazy look.
   c. The hazy look is known as *sfumato*.

   _____

   _____

10. a. Leonardo pursued studies in many other fields.
    b. The fields included mathematics, botany, and architecture. **[-ing]**
    c. He pursued his studies until his death in 1519.

    _____

    _____

Revising with Style

Combining Sentences IV

To improve the readability, variety, and style of your sentences, try combining them. One way to combine sentences is to take information from one sentence and embed it as a clause in another sentence. A **clause** is a group of words that contains a subject and a verb. You can use a clause in the same way you would use an adjective, an adverb, or a noun. The examples below show ways you can combine sentences by using adjective clauses, adverb clauses, or noun clauses.

- Use an adjective clause starting with *that, which, who, whom, whose, when* or *where*. Like an adjective, an adjective clause modifies a noun or a pronoun and should appear close to the noun or pronoun it modifies. Set off an adjective clause with commas only if it is not essential to the meaning of the sentence.
  a. Minnie Evans was an artist.
  b. She found painting as vital as breathing. **[who]**
  *Minnie Evans was an artist **who found painting as vital as breathing.***

- Use an adverb clause starting with a subordinating conjunction such as *before, after, until, whenever, although, if,* or *because*. Like an adverb, an adverb clause modifies a verb. If an adverb clause begins a sentence, set the clause off with a comma.
  a. She had no formal training. **[Although . . . ,]**
  b. She produced striking art.
  ***Although she had no formal training,** she produced striking art.*

- Use a noun clause starting with a subordinating word such as *that, who, whose, what, why, which, how, when,* or *where*. Like a noun, a noun clause can be used as a subject, an object, or a complement in a sentence and is not set off with commas.
  a. She dreamed something both at night and during the day.
  b. She painted pictures of it. **[what]**
  *She painted pictures of **what she dreamed both at night and during the day.***

EXERCISE Combine each cluster of sentences into a single sentence. Where indicated, use the underlined words and phrases and the bracketed words, word parts, and punctuation marks in your combined sentences.

Sample a. Minnie Eva Jones married Julius Evans.
  b. She was born in North Carolina in 1892. **[who]**
  c. She was only sixteen. **[when]**

Revision Minnie Eva Jones, who was born in North Carolina in 1892, married Julius Evans when she was only sixteen.

1. a. Minnie Evans was a child. **[Ever since . . . ,]**
  b. She had strange waking dreams.

_____

_____

Revising with Style

2. a. Her dreams were filled with fanciful creatures, intricate flowers, and mysterious faces.
   b. <u>She called</u> her dreams <u>"day visions."</u> **[, which . . . ,]**

   _____

   _____

3. a. Minnie's grandmother told her stories about their ancestors in Africa.
   b. <u>Minnie called</u> her grandmother <u>Mama Mary</u>. **[, whom . . . ,]**
   c. These stories inspired <u>her childhood drawings</u>. **[that]**

   _____

   _____

4. a. <u>Something</u> persuaded her to stop drawing. **[What]**
   b. <u>It was</u> the ridicule of her friends and the scorn of her teachers.

   _____

   _____

5. a. Minnie did not draw again for many years.
   b. <u>During</u> those years, <u>she married, raised three sons, and worked as a housekeeper</u>. **[which]**

   _____

   _____

6. a. <u>She was forty-three years old</u>. **[When . . . ,]**
   b. She couldn't ignore the vivid pictures in her head anymore.

   _____

   _____

7. a. She began to hang her paintings on the wall of the gatehouse at Airlie Gardens.
   b. <u>There</u> she was working as a collector of admission fees. **[, where]**

   _____

   _____

8. a. Minnie died at the age of ninety-five. **[Before . . . ,]**
   b. She had become a well-known and respected folk artist.
   c. She <u>never lost sight of her dreams</u>. **[who]**

   _____

   _____

Revising with Style

Using Transitions

To connect related ideas, use transitions. **Transitions** are words that help your writing flow from one idea to another. The chart below provides just a few examples of transitions you can use.

Common Transitions	
Time	first, when, until, next, before, finally, after, that night, meanwhile, then
Location	above, below, here, underneath, inside, there, in the distance
Importance	first, mainly, primarily, last, most important, secondly, next
Cause and Effect	as a result, because, consequently, since, therefore, then
Comparison	similarly, like, just as, also, in the same way, in addition, moreover
Contrast	although, but, even so, however, on the other hand, unlike, while

The following example shows how the flow of a paragraph can be improved by adding transitions. Notice that a transition may be appropriately used at the beginning, middle, or end of a sentence.

Without Transitions We tried to fly to Seattle. We wanted to see our favorite band perform. Thunderstorms passed through the region, and all flights were cancelled. All of the hotels near the airport were full. We had to sleep at the airport. We missed the concert. We were relieved not to fly during the storm.

With Transitions **Yesterday** we tried to fly to Seattle **because** we wanted to see our favorite band perform **there. But** thunderstorms passed through the region, and **as a result,** all flights were cancelled. **In addition,** all of the hotels near the airport were full. **Consequently,** we had to sleep at the airport. **Although** we missed the concert, we were relieved not to fly during the storm.

EXERCISE Using the transition type shown in the parentheses, rewrite one or both sentences in each pair to clarify their relationship. Combine the two sentences if you wish, omitting words or changing their forms as necessary.

Sample My friend Rebecca likes luxury vacations. I prefer adventure travel. (contrast)

Revision My friend Rebecca likes luxury vacations. However, I prefer adventure travel.

1. Rebecca and I count down the days until our vacations. Children count down the days until summer. (comparison)

_____

_____

Revising with Style

2. I go backpacking in remote places. Rebecca goes sunbathing where there are lots of people. (contrast)

_____

_____

3. I like to go backpacking. It's inexpensive. (cause and effect)

_____

_____

4. I like backpacking because it's affordable. It's fun. (comparison)

_____

_____

5. I hiked along the crest of the Appalachian Mountains. I could see miles of forest. (location)

_____

_____

6. I came back from all that hiking. I was in the best shape of my life. (time)

_____

_____

7. Improving my physical condition was only a minor benefit. I felt I'd accomplished something. (importance)

_____

_____

8. I was working up a sweat hiking. Rebecca was lying on a beach all day. (contrast)

_____

_____

9. She works as a personal trainer. She wants to take it easy for her vacation. (cause and effect)

_____

_____

10. Rebecca is on her feet all day at work. I sit at a desk. (contrast)

_____

_____

Revising with Style

Building Coherent Paragraphs I

To make sure your writing is coherent, check to see whether the sentences in each paragraph hang together logically. One logical way to organize your writing is by **chronological order**—that is, by presenting events in the order in which they occur. For example, if you're explaining how to bake a cake, your readers will want to follow along step by step. They don't want to get to the end of your recipe and read, "By the way, when you added the eggs earlier, you should have separated them first." Look at the following paragraph.

> When choosing a watermelon, remember these three steps. Check **first** to see whether the watermelon is firm, symmetrical, and free of dents and bruises. **Once** you've found a watermelon that looks good, pick it up to see if it feels heavy for its size. It should: a fresh, juicy watermelon is mostly water, which is heavy. **The last step** is to turn the watermelon over to make sure that it has a yellowish spot underneath. The spot is where the watermelon lay ripening in the sun.

See how the transitions clarify the order suggested by the topic sentence, which begins the paragraph. Note too that not all sentences in a chronologically ordered paragraph need transitions. Some flow naturally from preceding sentences.

EXERCISE The sentences in the following paragraphs are in the wrong order. Number each set of sentences to put them in chronological order.

Sample

__3__ Once they were cool, the baker decorated them with icing.

__2__ The baker then took the cookies out to let them cool.

__1__ The cookies in the baker's oven looked like they were ready.

Paragraph 1

_____ First, wash both the melon and the knife you'll be cutting with.

_____ With a fork, scrape the seeds from each strip and from the flesh left on the rind.

_____ Then cut the melon in half lengthwise and again in quarters.

_____ To de-seed a honeydew melon with a minimum of fuss, follow these few simple steps.

_____ Along the seed line of each quarter, cut off a strip of melon flesh and separate the strip from the rest of the melon.

Revising with Style

Paragraph 2

_____ While the sugar mixture is cooling, purée 5 pounds of melon, seeded and cut into 1-inch cubes, and put the purée in a large bowl.

_____ Finally, freeze the whisked mixture in the bowl and scoop out to serve.

_____ To make melon ice, first combine 3/4 cup of water and 1 cup of sugar in a medium saucepan and cook over high heat until the mixture boils.

_____ Next, pour the cooled sugar mixture into the melon purée, add 2 tablespoons of lime juice, and whisk thoroughly.

_____ Reduce the heat by half and stir until the sugar dissolves.

_____ When the sugar is entirely dissolved, remove the saucepan from the heat.

Revising with Style

Building Coherent Paragraphs II

To explain in a clear way why certain events occurred, organize your writing using **cause-and-effect order.** You might, for example, begin with one cause and then explain its several effects, or you might show how several causes led to a single effect. You may use a causal chain, as demonstrated in the paragraph below, to explain a more complex series of events, where one effect becomes the cause for another effect, and so on.

In 1746 James Lind, an English naval surgeon, noticed that on a ship with good water and provisions, 80 of 350 crew members developed scurvy—a disease whose symptoms include bleeding gums, anemia, and hemorrhaging. **To understand why this was happening,** Lind did an experiment. He divided twelve sick crew members into six groups. **By** preparing a different diet for each group, he found that those who were served lemons and oranges improved the most. Lind was **thus** convinced that eating citrus fruit was the best remedy. **In accordance with** Lind's findings, the British Admiralty eventually ordered lemon juice to be a part of naval rations. Scurvy virtually disappeared from the British fleet **as a result.**

Notice how the transitions, in bold, make clear how one idea leads to another. Also notice that transitions fit equally well at the beginning, middle, or end of a sentence.

EXERCISE The sentences in the following paragraphs are in the wrong order. Number each set of sentences to put them in cause-and-effect order.

Sample

___3___ Owing to the scientists' work, more recent research has now linked vitamins to the slowing of the aging process.

___1___ James Lind's experiments in the treatment of scurvy led to a theory of deficiency diseases.

___2___ From this theory, scientists early in the twentieth century were able to pinpoint vitamins as the key ingredients in preventing deficiency diseases.

Paragraph 1

_____ Because having an unpaired electron is unstable, a free radical either takes an electron from or gives an electron to a molecule in a nearby cell of the body.

_____ As a result of the deterioration, a person's body becomes aged and diseased.

_____ Free radicals, molecules that have one unpaired electron, regularly roam through a person's body.

_____ The cells deteriorate in turn from this disruption of their molecules.

Revising with Style

Paragraph 2

_____ Once in your blood or lymph system, the antioxidants render harmful free radicals in your body harmless.

_____ To ward off age and disease, eat foods high in antioxidants, such as broccoli and carrots.

_____ Moreover, because the cells are functioning properly, your body won't degenerate as quickly and you just might live longer.

_____ By eating these foods, you allow the antioxidants to enter your bloodstream or lymph system through your intestines.

_____ Since a smaller number of free radicals is left to attack your body's cells, the cells can continue to function properly.

Revising with Style

Building Coherent Paragraphs III

To describe rooms, vistas, objects, or scenes without confusing your reader, organize your paragraphs using spatial order. **Spatial order** makes clear where things are in relation to each other (and possibly to you, the writer). Using spatial order lets you not only connect ideas more clearly but also paint a picture with words, enabling readers to visualize the place you are describing. Study the paragraph below.

> If you ever visit Monticello, Thomas Jefferson's home, be sure to notice the special architectural details. **From** the Entrance Hall, you will notice **on your immediate left** a large rectangular fireplace. On closer inspection, you'll notice that **on either side** of it is a panel door. **Opening** either of these doors reveals a dumbwaiter, a contraption used to carry wine **up from** the cellar **below**. **Directly across from** the fireplace are two sets of sliding pocket doors that could keep out the cold from the tearoom **next to** the dining room **to the north.**

Notice how the boldfaced prepositional phrases and other transitions help you to visualize the place being described.

EXERCISE The sentences in the following paragraphs are in the wrong order. Number each set of sentences to put them in spatial order.

Sample

___2___ An old and cracked blender sat on the counter opposite me.

___3___ Next to it on the right was a toaster that looked like a refugee from the 1950s.

___1___ Upon entering the kitchen, I noticed two appliances on the counter.

Paragraph 1

_____ On the left, as you walk in, stands a whiter than white industrial-size refrigerator.

_____ With all the cooking power built into that stove, it's a wonder nothing Molly's family prepares ever burns.

_____ Between the refrigerator and a beautiful sink in the corner runs a clutterless countertop of gleaming stainless steel.

_____ My friend Molly's kitchen looks like a magazine spread.

_____ Across from the counter stands a bright red stove so imposing it looks like it could give a blast furnace competition.

_____ The counter can be clutterless because everything from knives to mixers fits in specially made cabinets underneath.

Revising with Style

Paragraph 2

_____ From the parked car, we could see that the house got plenty of shade from two trees, but not so much as to make the house seem dreary.

_____ In the real estate agent's car on the way to the house for sale, I could see that my parents were nervous with excitement.

_____ The agent fit the key in the lock, flung open the door, and waved us inside.

_____ While we stood on the front porch, the agent fumbled for the keys and explained that the house had just gone on the market.

_____ We pulled up to the curb directly in front of the house and sat there for a minute, staring at it.

_____ As we walked from the car up the stone-paved path to the front entrance, I could hear my parents say to each other, "Do you like it? Do you like it?"

Revising with Style

Building Coherent Paragraphs IV

In order to compare and contrast two subjects without confusing your readers, you need to organize your paragraphs effectively and use transition words to make the relationships between ideas and information clear. The chart below shows two methods of organizing comparison-contrast paragraphs: (1) by subject and (2) by feature.

Comparison-Contrast: Basketball and Baseball	
By Subject	**By Feature**
Subject 1: Basketball Feature A: Role of ball in scoring Feature B: Time factors Feature C: Skills required **Subject 2: Baseball** Feature A: Role of ball in scoring Feature B: Time factors Feature C: Skills required	**Feature A: Role of Ball in Scoring** Subject 1: Basketball Subject 2: Baseball **Feature B: Time factors** Subject 1: Basketball Subject 2: Baseball **Feature C: Skills Required** Subject 1: Basketball Subject 2: Baseball

The following paragraph organizes information by feature. The boldfaced words and phrases provide signal transitions that help make the comparison and contrast clear.

My favorite sports, basketball and baseball, are different in two key ways. **For one thing,** the ball is more important to scoring in basketball than it is in baseball. **Whereas** the only way to score in basketball is to get the ball through the hoop, in baseball, a player can score without the ball even being in play. A player can walk to first base and make it all the way to home plate by stealing bases and taking advantage of defensive errors and pop flies. **Another difference** between the two sports is the role that time plays in each. In basketball, play is divided into four quarters of specific duration. A team that is rallying to a comeback in the fourth quarter can almost be said to be playing against the clock as much as playing against the other team, since it has a limited time frame in which to score. **On the other hand,** baseball is not clocked: the game continues through nine innings, no matter how long those innings take. There is one important way in which basketball and baseball are similar, **however.** Each sport requires fast, athletic players who must be able to keep strategy in mind while making split-second decisions. That similarity must explain why I like both of these sports so much.

Try your hand at writing a comparison-contrast paragraph by completing the exercise on the following page. Use the chart above to help you plan a strategy for organizing your ideas.

Revising with Style

EXERCISE Use the information below to write a paragraph that compares and contrasts New York City with Los Angeles. Organize your paragraph by subject or by feature and be sure to include transition words and phrases to make your comparison and contrast clear. At the top of your paragraph, write *by subject* or *by feature* to indicate how you organized the information.

- Los Angeles covers 464 square miles.
- New York City, with a population of over seven million people, is the most populous city in the United States.
- New York City is culturally and ethnically diverse.
- New York City is one of the world's most important financial centers and is said to be the capital of publishing, fashion, and art in the United States.
- Los Angeles has a semitropical climate.
- In New York City, people usually walk, taxi, or take public transportation from place to place.
- The population of Los Angeles is made up of people from all over the world.
- In New York City, there are four distinct seasons.
- With a population of over three and a half million people, Los Angeles is the second largest city in the country.
- New York City covers 304 square miles.
- The vast majority of Los Angeles residents use private cars for transportation.
- Los Angeles is an important financial center and is the movie capital of the United States.

_____

_____

_____

_____

_____

_____

_____

_____

_____

_____

_____

_____

_____

_____

Revising with Style

Creating Unity in Paragraphs

Each paragraph you write should have **unity.** In other words, it should have a single focus, or main idea. When revising your paragraphs, be sure to look for a **topic sentence,** a statement of the main idea that often occurs at the beginning of a paragraph, as well as **supporting details,** sentences that clearly contribute to the main idea. In addition, watch out for paragraphs that discuss more than one main idea. If you notice a paragraph veering off onto a slightly different topic, you have probably found a good place to split the paragraph in two.

In the following example, notice how the sentences following the topic sentence at the beginning of the paragraph support the main idea.

Gertrude Stein once told the young writer Ernest Hemingway, "You are all a lost generation," and the term *lost generation* has been used again and again to describe the people of the post–World War I years. It describes those Americans, including Hemingway, who settled in Paris after the war because they were disillusioned with their home country. It also describes those who returned to the United States with an intense awareness of living in an unfamiliar, changing world.

EXERCISE A For each paragraph below, delete any sentence that does not support the main idea by drawing a line through it.

1. To see a rainbow, go outside when rain is falling but the sun is shining. Stand with your back to the sun. Your chances of spotting a rainbow are better in early morning or late afternoon, when the sun is low in the sky. Which time of day are you more alert? You're looking for sunlight refracted in and reflected off raindrops.

2. Ana de Osorio, the countess of Chinchon in Spain, moved to Peru with her husband in 1630. The people of Peru speak Spanish. While there, they both caught malaria. They were dosed with tree bark containing quinine, now known to cure malaria. When they returned home in 1638, the countess took some of the bark with her. They arrived to find Spain in the grip of a malaria epidemic. Ana gave the bark to her sick friends, ending the epidemic and saving many lives.

3. Nineteenth-century Americans went through wood at an alarming pace. They used it to build railroad ties, telegraph poles, bridges, and carriages. For example, ten miles of track were laid every day, which took about two thousand trees. They also burned it in quantity. Their fireplaces were very cozy. The railroads burned three thousand cords of wood for fuel every month.

4. In early nineteenth-century England, letter carriers had to collect payment from senders as they delivered the mail. This process really slowed them down. They didn't have a Pony Express. A man named Rowland Hill suggested prepaid delivery. In January 1840, the first letters carrying postage stamps were delivered. The stamps cost a penny apiece.

5. Anne Whitney was an American sculptor who lived from 1821 to 1915. She used her art to express her opinions on social issues, such as women's rights and the abolition of slavery. Slavery is a moral outrage. For example, to express her sympathies for the impoverished peasants of Rome, she made a statue that showed the goddess of Rome looking old, depressed, and weary.

Revising with Style

EXERCISE B Revise the following passage for better unity and focus by dividing it into paragraphs. Insert a paragraph symbol (¶) wherever a new paragraph should begin.

Teens recognize that the Internet has some problems. One of the biggest is the digital divide—the gap between people who have access to the Web and those who do not. At the moment, fewer than half of all teens have access from home. Many teens are optimistic about this issue, though. They point out that computers are becoming less expensive and many Internet service providers are free. These teens hope that one day soon, everyone will have access to the Internet, no matter what their income. The Internet has other problems. Some teens say they are worried about computer fraud and criminal hacking. Others are concerned about the possibility of Internet addiction. In one survey, twenty-eight percent of teen respondents said they spend more than twenty hours per week online (compared with sixteen percent of adult respondents). Still other teens fear that people will stop interacting in person. "The advances of the computer have already begun to create a more impersonal society," says fifteen-year-old Amanda Cannata. However, for most teens, the attitude seems to be full speed ahead. "Teens are most open to the possibilities of the Web," concludes author Mimi Mandel. "It's second nature to them, like television is to my generation."

Revising with Style

Understanding Elaboration

To tell a good story, give clear directions, or make someone you disagree with see your side of the argument, you will need to do more than give general ideas. You will need to give specific information. You will need to support your ideas with descriptive details, examples, anecdotes, facts, or statistics. In other words, you will need to **elaborate.**

In the first example below, the writer simply makes a claim without providing any true elaboration. The revised passage is more convincing because it includes two points that support the writer's claim: a fact (or valid observation), and a personal anecdote (or brief story).

Unelaborated Idea	Our school should set aside money in its budget to fund a magazine that publishes student writing and artwork. Students want this kind of magazine.
Elaborated Idea	Our school should set aside money in its budget to fund a magazine that publishes student writing and artwork. Although many students, either through class assignments or on their own initiative, write stories and poems, paint, draw, and photograph, they don't have a place to exhibit their work. Because I'm not enrolled in an art class, for example, no one at school can see the photographs I take in my spare time. A school-sponsored arts magazine would enable me to share my work with others.

EXERCISE Each passage below contains a type of elaboration. Read each passage carefully and identify the type of elaboration it contains by writing *descriptive details, examples, anecdotes, facts,* or *statistics,* on the line that follows. A passage may contain more than one type of elaboration. Underline the words and phrases in the passage that provide elaboration.

Sample   I understand the arguments against wearing fur and have decided to wear one anyway. Not only does fur solve, more efficiently than any other substance known to man, the need for warmth, it has also been with us for hundreds if not thousands of years.

Yona Zeldis McDonough, "Sisters Under the Skin"

Answer   I understand the arguments against wearing fur and have decided to wear one anyway. <u>Not only does fur solve, more efficiently than any other substance known to man, the need for warmth, it has also been with us for hundreds if not thousands of years.</u>

Facts

1. There is one profound difference between heroin and nicotine addiction. Tobacco kills 80 times as many people in this country. About 320,000 Americans die every year as a result of using tobacco products, while 4,000 die from the effects of heroin and related drugs.

Anthony Lewis, "Merchants of Death"

_____

Revising with Style

2. Are power rackets good for tennis? The weekend player has certainly benefited from them. Their large "sweet spot" can compensate for poor vision, awkward footwork, and lapses in concentration.

Mark Mathabane, "A Plague on Tennis"

_____

3. Fashions in names seem as arbitrary as fashions in carpet. One day everyone wants orange shag, then suddenly it's green berber.

Janet Simons, "The Name Reign: New Parents Balance the Trendy and Unique"

_____

4. Yet to understand just how different this place is, one has to see a "normal" coffee shop, such as the one in the modernistic building of concrete and glass that we visited the same day. Inside neon lights flicker, casting a ghostly light on the aluminum tables and chairs covered with plastic.

Slavenka Drakulić, "Pizza in Warsaw, Torte in Prague"

_____

5. Eager to counter the many charges of vacuousness and puffery that have plagued it, MTV has also aired public service programs about political, social, and environmental issues, even winning a prestigious Peabody Award for its two-hour retrospective on the '80s, "Decade."

George Varga, "Is It MTV, or Is It 'Empty-V'?"

_____

Revising with Style

Elaborating to Persuade

To persuade readers to agree with your opinions and possibly to take action, you will have to do more than simply state your opinion. You will have to provide information that supports your opinion—information in the form of details, facts, statistics, examples, or anecdotes. You will have to present new ideas and explain them in fully developed paragraphs. In short, you will have to **elaborate.**

How to Elaborate an Idea
1. State your claim.
2. Extend your idea with a piece of information.
3. Add one or two more relevant pieces of information.
4. Include a statement that explains or furthers your claim in light of the added information.

The type of elaboration you choose will depend on your subject. Notice how the unelaborated idea below is made more persuasive with the addition of examples.

Unelaborated idea   Students who ride the bus to school should be given beepers that let them know when the bus will reach their stop. They could use such a device.

Elaborated idea   Students who ride the bus to school should be given beepers that let them know when the bus will reach their stop. Although the bus is supposed to have a schedule, it rarely arrives on time because of traffic. Once, during a snowstorm this past winter, the bus was over half an hour late. Since I had to wait outside the whole time, I ended up catching a cold. If the bus had been able to beep me a few minutes before it arrived, I could have kept warm in my house and stayed healthy.

EXERCISE Revise each idea below by writing a well-elaborated paragraph. Use facts, examples, reasons, anecdotes, or other information to support the viewpoint presented. Continue your answers on your own paper if you need more space to write.

1. Town developers should use the site vacated by the old factory to create a municipal park, not a new mall. We have a mall already. Isn't one enough?

_____

_____

_____

_____

_____

Revising with Style

2. Students who wish to go to the prom only to dance should not be forced to buy tickets to the dinner beforehand. They want to dance, not eat.

_____

_____

_____

_____

_____

3. The school year has become too long; our principal should shorten it.

_____

_____

_____

_____

_____

4. If a desired course is not offered at our school, qualified students should be allowed to take it at a local community college instead. The students are qualified, aren't they?

_____

_____

_____

_____

_____

5. Parents and teachers are debating whether to open the school library during after-school hours. Though keeping it open will surely cost money, it's worth the expense. The library will be open longer, and that's a good thing.

_____

_____

_____

_____

_____

Revising with Style

Finding Your Voice

The term *voice* is often used to distinguish between active and passive verbs, but your voice as a writer has nothing to do with grammar. Read the lists below to help you understand what voice is and is not.

Your voice as a writer is . . .

- the sound of your writing that is unique to you—like your speaking voice
- a reflection of your values, beliefs, and attitudes
- that quality that makes your words ring true
- an honest and engaging expression of what you want to say

Your voice as a writer is not . . .

- a particular style, tone, or mood of writing
- an imitation of another writer's sound
- the sound of your writing when you are trying to show off how well you write
- a consistent use of a particular set of words or sentence structures

For an example of writing that strongly conveys a voice, read the following paragraph from "A Christmas Memory" by Truman Capote.

> Life separates us. Those who Know Best decide that I belong in a military school. And so follows a miserable succession of bugle-blowing prisons, grim reveille-ridden summer camps. I have a new home too. But it doesn't count. Home is where my friend is, and there I never go.

In this paragraph, Capote has a distinctive, almost poetic way of expressing a wry, melancholic view of the world.

The challenge you face as a writer is to find your own voice—and then to feel comfortable with it, develop it, and allow your writing to reflect it. Your voice cannot be learned. It can only be discovered.

EXERCISE A Circle the best answer to each of the following questions.

1. Which of the following must be present in any piece of writing for it to truly reflect the writer's voice?

   A. good grammar
   B. honesty
   C. humor

2. Which of the following standard pieces of advice for writers is most applicable to developing a writing voice?

   A. Write about what you know.
   B. Vary your sentence structure.
   C. Consider who your audience is.

Revising with Style

3. Which of the following statements would most likely describe a story in which your voice as a writer emerges?

   A. It is a story you feel you must tell.
   B. It is a popular kind of story—one that people almost always enjoy.
   C. It is a story that resembles the work of your favorite writer.

4. Imagine giving a piece of writing to a good friend to read. Which of the following responses would best indicate that the work reflects your voice?

   A. "I understand this completely and agree with every word."
   B. "This is amazingly good; I had no idea you could write so well."
   C. "If I hadn't already known, I would have guessed you had written this."

5. In which of the following circumstances would someone's writing most likely reflect his or her voice?

   A. taking a test
   B. writing a diary entry
   C. writing a set of instructions

EXERCISE B Rewrite each passage below in your own voice. Change sentence structures and add, replace, or take away words and punctuation as necessary. Continue your answers on your own paper if you need more space to write.

Sample   The first Latin Grammy Awards presentation was on April 13, 2000. The awards are open to international competition and reflect the growth of the Latin music market. Any musician who records in Spanish or Portuguese is eligible for nomination.

Revision   Finally, on April 13, 2000, recognition of the growing importance of Latin music came in the form of the first-ever Latin Grammy Awards presentation. Proving that Latin music is an international, multicultural phenomenon, competition for the award is open to any artist in the world who records in Spanish or Portuguese. Latin music's time has come.

1. In 1998 Mark McGwire, first baseman for the St. Louis Cardinals, surpassed the single-year home run record set by Roger Maris of the New York Yankees in 1961. McGwire hit seventy home runs. Maris hit sixty-one.

_____

_____

_____

2. An increase in the minimum wage could benefit the education of teenagers who work after school. If Congress were to pass legislation increasing teenagers' wages, teenagers could reduce the number of hours they work and increase the time they spend on study or extracurricular activities.

_____

_____

_____

Revising with Style

Identifying Metaphors, Similes, and Personification

You can add color and emphasis to your writing by using **figurative language**—language that is used for descriptive effect. Instead of being literally true, figurative language expresses a truth that extends beyond the literal level in a fresh and original way. To create an effective figure of speech—such as a metaphor, a simile, or personification—ask yourself, "What does this remind me of?" Study the definitions and models taken from literature below.

A **simile** is a figure of speech that uses the word *like* or *as* to compare two seemingly unlike things.

- In the darkness, Mr. Shiflet's smile stretched like a weary snake waking up by a fire.

  Flannery O'Connor, "The Life You Save May Be Your Own"

A **metaphor** is a figure of speech in which two seemingly unlike things are compared without using the word *like* or *as*. A metaphor can help readers vividly perceive the first item in the comparison by suggesting a similarity that underlies its relationship to the second.

- Truth is a hard deer to hunt.   Stephen Vincent Benét, "By the Waters of Babylon"

Personification is a figure of speech that gives a human quality to an animal, an object, a force of nature, or an idea.

- The hour had crept toward midnight.   Loren Eiseley, "The Angry Winter"

EXERCISE A Identify the type of figurative language used in each sentence as *simile, metaphor,* or *personification.*

Sample ___*simile*___	My love is like a bubble.
1._____	His face was shaped like a trapezoid.
2._____	The sun was a bowl overturned.
3._____	With a scythe in his hands, Death haunted her dreams.
4._____	That old car is as big as a boat.
5._____	My keyboard is an obstacle course.
6._____	When the virus was launched, the World Wide Web frayed.
7._____	Your explanation is as clear as cream.
8._____	Her smile lights up a room like a sodium lamp.
9._____	Mother Nature is not happy right now.
10._____	Sometimes I think Jason is a book without pages.

Revising with Style

EXERCISE B Rewrite each sentence, using the figure of speech indicated in parentheses to make the sentence more interesting and engaging. Omit or change words, phrases, and punctuation as necessary.

Sample   The sound of her laughter rings out. (use simile)
Revision   Her laughter rings out like the tiny bells on a charm bracelet.

1. The airplane spiraled overhead. (use simile)

_____

_____

2. White sheets billowed on the clothesline. (use simile)

_____

_____

3. The water of the lake was very clear. (use simile)

_____

_____

4. The immigrants were sworn in as citizens; the Statue of Liberty was nearby. (personify the Statue of Liberty)

_____

_____

5. The road bends and curves through the forest. (personify the road)

_____

_____

6. Playing the guitar takes me to other cultures. (use metaphor)

_____

_____

7. The skateboarders twirled in midair. (use simile)

_____

_____

8. A multitude of ants came into our kitchen. (personify the ants)

_____

_____

Revising with Style

Identifying Hyperbole and Understatement

To add humor to your writing or to focus your readers' attention, use hyperbole or understatement. Hyperbole and understatement are two sides of the same coin: they both use distortion to make a point. **Hyperbole** is a figure of speech that makes something seem bigger or more important than it really is. It uses exaggeration to express strong emotion, emphasize a point, or evoke humor. **Understatement** is language that makes something seem less important than it really is. Look at the following examples.

| Hyperbole | It rained enough yesterday to float a steel mill. |
| Understatement | You might say Albert Einstein had a good head for numbers. |

Like stand-up comics or writers of **satire**—a form of persuasion that uses humor to criticize and change society—you can use hyperbole and understatement to skewer your target, whether it be a social practice or institution, a political plan, or a human quirk. Just don't overuse these strategies, or they will lose their effectiveness.

EXERCISE A Label each item as *hyperbole* or *understatement* in the space provided.

Sample _____hyperbole_____ I've told you a million times not to call me during my favorite show.

1. _____ Sally was a tad annoyed when her brother sneaked a peak at her secret diary.

2. _____ "The weather *is* brisk," Nathan admitted, as the thermometer read minus ten degrees Fahrenheit.

3. _____ That hotel room was so small that even the mice had hunched shoulders.

4. _____ "Oh, I've been known to bang out a chord or two," said the renowned concert pianist.

5. _____ Every word Laurie says is a lie, including "a" and "the."

6. _____ You must admit, Ken isn't the most talented singer in the world.

7. _____ I've wanted to go to France since the beginning of time.

8. _____ Herbert doesn't actually brush his teeth; he just waves a toothbrush near his mouth.

9. _____ How ugly is that shirt? Well, if you paid more than a nickel for it, you were ripped off.

10. _____ Maya was somewhat pleased when she aced the calculus final.

Revising with Style

EXERCISE B Rewrite each sentence to make it either hyperbolic or understated (your choice). Change words, phrases, or punctuation as needed.

Sample The gardens at Winterthur are beautiful.

Revision The gardens at Winterthur are the most beautiful things I've ever seen.
or
The gardens at Winterthur are pleasant enough.

1. I enjoy playing basketball.

_____

2. Dave's sand castle was big.

_____

3. Dennis was thrilled when the Steelers won the Super Bowl.

_____

4. The Marquez family seems to have a lot of money.

_____

5. Jessica isn't getting enough sleep; she fell asleep at the lunch table today.

_____

6. When Amy wore her alligator shoes, she attracted attention.

_____

7. For me, cleaning house is an unpleasant activity.

_____

8. Video games can be time-consuming.

_____

9. People who talk on the phone while they drive do not pay enough attention to the road.

_____

10. Mark was very disappointed about getting a D on the test.

_____

11. Lilacs smell sweet.

_____

12. Books are stacked four feet high around the perimeter of Stephen's room.

_____

Revising with Style

Identifying Errors in Logic

Whether writing an editorial or a persuasive speech, be sure to avoid **logical fallacies,** or errors in logic. Logic is the process of clear and organized thinking that leads to a reasonable conclusion. Errors in logic weaken your argument and your credibility. Although using errors in logic may persuade readers who don't catch the errors, readers who do may likely dismiss your entire argument. Study the examples in the chart below.

Common Errors in Logic	
Stereotyping	You should remind Grandma about her appointment. Old people are very forgetful.
False Analogy	To prevent shoplifting, we ought to ban kids under eighteen from shopping together. There are hardly any children in a retirement community, and shoplifting rarely occurs there.
Loaded Language	Even good kids can get caught up in a mob mentality whenever they gang together with other mall rats.
Limited Sample	Shoplifters always wear baggy clothing. This is what a classmate of mine did.
False Cause	When Melissa wasn't getting good grades, her parents gave her a curfew. Her grades later improved. It's clear that the curfew helped her do better in school.

EXERCISE For each item below, identify the error in logic as *stereotyping, false analogy, loaded language, limited sample,* or *false cause.*

Sample _____loaded language_____ Mr. Anton must be a lunatic to believe that life could exist in other galaxies.

1. _____ Ever since we started using filtered water, I've noticed that my headaches have disappeared. Something in the tap water must have been giving me headaches.

2. _____ Little Louie is the sweetest, most agreeable toddler in town; I simply can't imagine that he would ever give his parents a hard time.

3. _____ My daughter told me that she was studying with your daughter last night, but I don't believe her. Teens are dishonest with their parents.

4. _____ If parents are strict, their children won't get into trouble. Look at Calvin's Hill Military Academy. Students at that school rarely get into trouble because the students there learn discipline.

Revising with Style

5. _____ The stricter the parents, the more trouble their children get into. For example, I once knew some obsessively strict parents whose child wound up stealing cars.

6. _____ The mayor believed that lining the city streets with artwork would bolster tourism, and he was right. Ever since the artwork was put in place, I've seen more people who look like tourists walking around.

7. _____ If our school had more students, we'd have a better softball team. Lawndale High has more students, and its tennis, soccer, and swim teams all went to state championships this year.

8. _____ I'd love to go camping with you at Gray Lake, but I'll get bitten all over by mosquitoes if I go. A friend of mine went there a month ago, and he suffered terribly from mosquito bites.

9. _____ My history teacher shouldn't torture our class with so much busy work. Last week, he assigned a ton of reading, and hardly any of the material appeared on this week's quiz.

10. _____ You want to do volunteer work in Central America before going to college? You must be a vegetarian, then. All volunteer workers are vegetarians.

Revising with Style

Avoiding Clichés and Sexist Language

As you revise your writing, keep an eye out for clichés and sexist language. Replacing them will make your prose clearer, more interesting, and less offensive to your readers.

Clichés are stale and overused expressions. Some of them may at one time have been apt metaphors or expressions, but through overuse they've lost their meaning. Here are a few examples of clichés:

Clichés		
after all is said and done	good as gold	few and far between
cute as a button	right as rain	sad but true

By using **sexist language**—phrasing specific to one gender when either or both can apply—you run the risk of excluding and annoying many of your readers. Be careful to replace sexist words like *stewardess* and *mailman* with gender-neutral terms like *flight attendant* and *mail carrier*. Also, avoid using male pronouns to refer to antecedents of unknown or mixed gender. Here are some ways you can effectively recast a sentence that has sexist language.

Gender-specific	Each student turned in **his** paper
Gender-neutral	Each student turned in **a** paper.
	Each student turned in **his or her** paper.
	All the **students** turned in **their** papers.

EXERCISE A For each sentence below, underline the cliché(s). If the sentence uses sexist language, write *sexist* in the space provided.

Sample _____sexist_____ Each actor was as cool as a cucumber when he spoke his lines.

1. _____ Any writer worth his salt considers his audience.

2. _____ Aunt Helen is a poetess who specializes in tugging at readers' heartstrings.

3. _____ Quantum physics, the study of atomic particles, is not for the faint of heart.

4. _____ Lonny is true blue, but his brother Lenny is a snake in the grass.

5. _____ Any real gardener is proud of his green thumb.

Revising with Style

EXERCISE B Rewrite each sentence, replacing clichés with original phrases and sexist language with nonsexist language. Not all sentences have both clichés and sexist language.

Sample   Each actor was as cool as a cucumber when he spoke his lines.
Revision   *The actors exuded confidence when they spoke their lines.*

1. Every engineer at the conference brought his visual aids.

_____

2. Firemen risk their lives every day putting out fires.

_____

3. On our flight to San Francisco, the stewardesses were very helpful.

_____

4. My cousin Chris is as strong as a horse.

_____

5. Every athlete at the Olympics represents his country with pride.

_____

6. A registered nurse makes use of her training with every patient she sees.

_____

7. Abel passed his driving exam with flying colors.

_____

8. The waitress apologized for mixing up our orders.

_____

9. A research scientist chooses his career path based on his interests.

_____

10. When Jamal bumped his head on that pipe, he saw stars.

_____

Revising with Style

Proofreading I

After you've written and revised a draft, be sure that it's free of errors that may distract your readers. **Proofreading** is the final check you make before sharing your writing with others. Read each word and sentence several times, checking for specific errors. Make sure you've followed the rules for capitalization below.

- Capitalize the first word in every sentence.
  My sister loves to read horror stories. **N**ot everyone does.

- Capitalize the first word of a direct quotation that is a sentence, but don't capitalize the first word of a quotation that is not a sentence.
  She said, "**W**hy don't you try this novel?" A reviewer called it a "**n**ail-biter."

- Capitalize the pronoun *I*.
  But **I** told her **I** don't like blood and gore.

- Capitalize proper nouns (nouns that name a specific person, place, thing, or event).
  Then **M**r. **M**iller, my neighbor, recommended a short story by **S**hirley **J**ackson.

- Capitalize proper adjectives (adjectives formed from proper nouns).
  She was an **A**merican writer who lived in Vermont.

- Capitalize key words in titles of books, articles, songs, movies, TV shows, and so on.
  The story is called "**T**he **L**ottery."

- Capitalize words showing family relationships only when substituting them for names.
  My friend Becky's **d**ad agrees with Cindy. So does **M**om.

EXERCISE Correct any errors in capitalization by drawing a slash (/) through a capital letter that should be lowercase and three lines (≡) under a lowercase letter that should be capitalized.

Sample   i've started reading fantasy/Science Fiction writers, like sheri tepper and orson scott Card.

1. one of my favorite Fantasy writers is esther friesner.

2. friesner was born in new york city in 1951.

3. Her parents both taught in the brooklyn school system; her Mother taught English and her Father taught spanish, latin, italian, and algebra.

4. "I liked to Write at an early age," said friesner. "in fact, I started making stories when i was three."

5. the first writing she ever sold was an article for *cats* magazine.

6. Many of her early Stories were rejected by Isaac asimov's Magazine.

7. Freisner kept trying and has now published more than twenty Novels, starting with *Mustapha and his wise dog*.

8. Reviewer fred lerner wrote in *Voice of youth advocates* that Friesner is "One of the funniest" writers of fantasy fiction.

Revising with Style

Proofreading II

Use an apostrophe to indicate the possessive form of nouns and pronouns, the plural form of letters and figures, and the omission of letters and figures. Never use it to make a word plural. When you proofread your writing, make sure that you've followed the rules for apostrophes listed below.

- Use an apostrophe and -s to form the possessive of a singular noun (even one that ends in -s).
  the book**'s** cover   the glas**s's** fingerprints   Dorothy Sayer**s's** novels

- Use an apostrophe alone to form the possessive of a plural noun that ends in -s. Make sure the apostrophe follows the -s.
  the Smith**s'** house   the classe**s'** tests   the detective**s'** cases

- Use an apostrophe and -s to form the possessive of a plural noun that does not end in -s.
  children**'s** books   women**'s** clothing   the deer**'s** trail

- Use an apostrophe and -s to form the possessive of a singular indefinite pronoun.
  one**'s** book   everybody**'s** alibi

- Put only the last word of a compound noun in the possessive form.
  my sister-in-law**'s** library card   the surgeon general**'s** warning

- If two or more people possess something jointly, use the possessive form only for the last person named. If two or more people possess something individually, put each one's name in the possessive form.
  Don and Barbara**'s** party   Don**'s** and Barbara**'s** schedules

- Use an apostrophe and -s to form the plural of letters, numerals, symbols, and words used to represent themselves. (Underline or italicize except for -'s.)
  all *A*'s   four *6*'s   @'s   too many *the*'s

- Use an apostrophe in place of letters omitted in contractions. (A contraction is a word made up of two words that have been combined by omission of one or more letters.)
  I + am = I'm   you + are = you're   Dave + is = Dave's

- Use an apostrophe in place of the omitted numerals of a specific year.
  the earthquake of '92   the World Series of '68   the summer of '01

EXERCISE A Use the proofreading symbol (ⱽ) to add apostrophes where needed. Use the delete symbol (ℐ) to cross out apostrophes used incorrectly. If the sentence is correct, write C in the space provided.

Sample _____ Some mystery novels plot's are predictable.

1. _____ Many people consider Edgar Allan Poes short story "The Murder's in the Rue Morgue," published in 1841, the first detective story.

2. _____ His detective, Auguste Dupin, used clear thinking to figure out who committed the murders.

Revising with Style

3. _____ Arthur Conan Doyles Sherlock Holmes was another famous literary detective.

4. _____ Holmeses' specialty was to solve every crime by detailed reasoning, and he always minded his ps and qs.

5. _____ In the 1900s, Mary Roberts Rinehart and G. K. Chestertons writing careers began.

6. _____ The 20s saw Agatha Christie's first novels, featuring Hercule Poirots sleuthing, which couldnt have been more entertaining to readers'.

7. _____ Do you prefer Raymond Chandlers journeys down the mean streets' of Los Angeles to Joyce Carol Oates psychological studies?

8. _____ Tony Hillerman's novels take readers inside the lives of the Navajo Tribal Police.

9. _____ Nevada Barrs career as a national park ranger wasnt wasted when she began a mystery series who'se hero, Anna Pigeon, is a park ranger.

10. _____ Especially popular today are detectives who understand the inner workings of mens' and womens' minds.

EXERCISE B Use the proofreading symbol (ⱽ) to add apostrophes where needed. Use the delete symbol (ꝫ) to cross out apostrophes used incorrectly.

Sample My parents were pleased that I got four As this semester.

1. Did you hear Keisha say, "Im hosting a party at my aunts house"?

2. Leonardo and Fidels father owns an electronics repair shop.

3. Arthur and Lisas math classes are using the same textbook.

4. Everyones participation is needed to guarantee the success of the schools drive for coats' and shoes for the homeless.

5. Were constantly reminded of the old adage "You cant judge a book by it's cover."

6. All the family enjoyed listening to Great-Grandfathers stories about the blizzard of 88—that's 1888, of course.

7. The business partner's were aware that they needed a formal contract, not merely a "gentlemans agreement."

8. The campers couldn't believe that they were lost in spite of following their leaders directions to the campsite and her advice to bring a compass.

9. The twins summer jobs in their brother-in-laws store left them little time to enjoy water sports at their parents cottage.

10. The students objection to the schools uniform policy doesnt give them the right to ignore it.

Name ______________________________ Date ______________

Revising with Style

LESSON 37

Proofreading III

Commas clarify meaning. When proofreading your work, be sure that you follow the rules below.

- Use serial commas to separate three or more words, phrases, or clauses in a sentence, except when all the items are connected by conjunctions.
  Good fiction manages to entertain, to inform, and to move readers.
  Science fiction and mystery and romance are all genres of fiction.
- Use commas to set off nonessential elements (participial phrases, infinitive phrases, adjective clauses, and appositives that are not essential to the sentence's meaning).
  The storyteller, having finished, waited for her audience to applaud. (nonessential participial phrase)
  The storyteller wearing the red dress was the scariest. (essential participial phrase)
- Use commas to set off interjections (such as *oh* and *well*), parenthetical expressions (such as *in fact* and *on the other hand*), and conjunctive adverbs (such as *however* and *consequently*).
  Well, I didn't know that you had published a story!
- Use a comma after a long or potentially confusing introductory prepositional phrase.
  In awarding prizes for literature, judges often look for authors with distinctive writing styles. (long prepositional phrase)
  After the voting, results are secret until they are announced. (confusing prepositional phrase)
- Use a comma after an introductory participle or participial phrase.
  Feeling faint from excitement, he sat down quickly.
- Use commas to set off introductory adverb clauses and internal adverb clauses that interrupt the sentence's flow.
  Because he had spent years writing his book, the author needed the prize money.
  The author, because he had spent years writing his book, needed the prize money.

EXERCISE A Use the proofreading symbol (^) to add commas as needed in the sentences below. Use the delete symbol (⌀) to cross out commas used incorrectly.

Sample Fortunately,^ I had my raincoat with me.

1. More often than ideals economics fuel revolutions.

2. In France for example extreme poverty resulted in the French Revolution a conflict between economic and social classes.

3. As for the American Revolution it stemmed partly from taxation without representation.

4. Early in the conflict angry colonists disguised as Native Americans and wielding hatchets boarded British ships and tossed their cargo of tea into Boston Harbor.

5. Many colonists, who owned or could obtain a weapon, helped fight the British.

Revising with Style

6. The British troops who were reputed to be a fine fighting force made easy targets for the muskets of the ragtag colonial militia.

7. While the colonists fought their wives maintained their farms and businesses.

8. Valley Forge where Washington's troops wintered, during the American Revolution is located in Pennsylvania.

9. The early patriots had wisdom courage and determination.

10. Having sacrificed to make a better life in the New World they would not surrender to the demands of Great Britain.

11. After winning the Revolutionary War the colonists faced the difficult tasks of forming a new government and developing an unfamiliar country.

12. The pioneers who settled the West struggled to build homes to cultivate the land and to defend themselves against hostile forces.

13. When American farmers pushed westward they caused resentment in those who owned ranches or herded cattle for a living.

14. The Mexican War begun in 1846 was an attempt to settle a border dispute.

15. One of the battle sites, was the Alamo a venerable old Spanish mission.

EXERCISE B Use the proofreading symbol (⁁) to insert commas as needed in the following sentences. Use the delete symbol (⤷) to cross out commas used incorrectly.

Sample A quarter, a comb, and a big ball of lint, were all I had left in my pocket.

1. Because the weather was atypically cold few people could enjoy summer sports such as swimming boating and picnicking.

2. On the Fourth of July however everyone in our family had a marvelous time.

3. We made a festive picnic lunch which we ate, in the den.

4. A softball game involving children teenagers and adults, provided fun and exercise in the afternoon.

5. As soon as dusk fell we got ready to watch the fireworks and oh were they spectacular!

6. In my opinion the fireworks display as beautiful as it was could have been longer.

7. Although, we had enjoyed ourselves we were not ready to end the day's activities.

8. Putting on sweaters and light jackets we walked to the ice cream shop where we bought our favorite desserts.

9. With our hands full of good things, to eat we hurried back home.

10. Huddling together in the den we watched a scary exciting movie.

Name _____   Date _____

Revising with Style   LESSON 38

Proofreading IV

There are a number of rules pertaining to the use of commas in writing. When proofreading, be sure that you follow the rules in the list below.

- Use a comma between the main clauses and before the coordinating conjunction in a compound sentence.

  Agatha Christie was a commercially successful writer, **and** she was often praised by critics.

- Place a comma between coordinate adjectives that precede a noun. (To test whether the adjectives are coordinate, try reversing their order or putting *and* between them. If the sentence sounds unnatural, the adjectives are not coordinate and commas shouldn't be used. Generally, adjectives that describe shape, age, and material do not need to be separated by commas.)

  An interesting, thought-provoking, touching book is *The Giver* by Lois Lowry.
  A big old bloodhound howled at the moon. (*not* coordinate adjectives)

- Use commas to set off titles when they follow a person's name; the various parts of an address, a geographical term, or a complete date; and the parts of a reference that cite the exact source.

  Lucy Patel, M.D. (*but* Dr. Lucy Patel)
  My cousin lives at 1275 Sloan Avenue, Latrobe, PA 15650.
  The bookstore in Oakmont, Iowa, opened on Saturday, May 27, 2000.
  (*but* The bookstore opened in May 2000; the exact date was May 27.)
  John Milton mentions the snake in *Paradise Lost*, book 9, line 643.

- Use commas to set off words or names used when you address someone directly.

  Have you read any books by Jean Fritz, Marty?
  Yes, my friend, I read her memoir.

- Use a comma to set off a tag question, which implies an answer to the question preceding it.

  You like memoirs, don't you?

- Use a comma after the salutation of an informal letter and after the closing of all letters.

  Dear Nikko,   Dear Uncle Fred,   Dear Grandma,
  Sincerely,   Cordially,   Yours truly,

EXERCISE A Use the proofreading symbol (∧) to add commas as needed in the sentences below.

Sample   You're doing well∧aren't you?

1. The school library has a wide selection of books by modern American authors doesn't it?

2. The neighborhood library moved to its new site on September 1 1999.

3. Lorraine have you ever visited the city's central library?

Revising with Style   **79**

Revising with Style

4. The librarian gave me the address of the House of Representatives in Washington D.C.

5. Will you be in Washington when Congress is in session Melanie or will you be there during the annual recess?

EXERCISE B Use the proofreading symbol (⌃) to add commas as needed in the letter below. Use the delete symbol (⌿) to cross out commas used incorrectly. Some sentences contain more than one error; some contain none.

> 2054 Sunset Place
>
> Brookhaven MN 56587
>
> August 5 2001

Dear Ruth Ellen

I'm sorry I haven't written but I'm answering your letter now before you become Ruth Ellen Carson M.D. As you might have guessed, I've been really busy. For my social studies class our group is polling voters in the school elections. That is we're asking people ahead of time whom they're planning to vote for. We've chosen a representative sample of students and every week we check in with them. This project uses our people skills our math skills and our computer skills. You can imagine how time-consuming it is can't you?

Taking up the rest of my time, is reading which I still love. I've been especially interested in biographies, and autobiographies. Among my favorites are books by Jill Ker Conway Jean Fritz and Russell Baker. Daniel Pinkwater has a fascinating, insightful hilarious memoir called *Chicago Days/Hoboken Nights.* He's a writer, who always makes me laugh.

I'm sending you a review about an anthology of essays called *The Autobiographical Eye.* I haven't found the book yet but the review appeared on page 3, of the *Donegal Bulletin* on April 7 2000. I remember that fiction is your first love so perhaps you will enjoy reading about the lives loves and inspirations of some of your favorite fiction writers.

> Sincerely
>
> Jared

Revising with Style

Proofreading V

When proofreading your writing, check to see that every sentence ends with an appropriate punctuation mark. There are three punctuation marks you can use at the end of a sentence: a period, an exclamation point, or a question mark.

- Use a period to end a declarative sentence and a polite command.
  I like to read books and magazines about the sciences. (declarative sentence)
  Please hand me that magazine. (polite command)

- Use an exclamation point to show strong feeling or indicate a forceful command.
  Oh, how I'd like to ride the space shuttle someday! (exclamation)
  Stop that! (strong command)

- Use a question mark to indicate a direct question.
  Are you interested in astronomy?

- Don't use a question mark after a declarative sentence that contains an indirect question.
  Diane asked whether you were interested in astronomy.

EXERCISE Add a period, exclamation point, or question mark at the end of each sentence.

Sample   There are many areas of science that interest me

Revision   There are many areas of science that interest me.

1. Have you heard of Rachel Carson

2. She has been called the mother of the environmental movement

3. This biologist was one of the first people to see that we were poisoning our environment

4. The warnings in her book *Silent Spring* are so frightening

5. Don't you agree that physics is another interesting scientific field

6. Researchers in this field study the behavior of galaxies as well as particles smaller than atoms

7. Who doesn't have a desire to understand the way the universe works

8. In his book *The Elegant Universe,* physicist Brian Greene asks questions about how the universe began and whether time travel is possible

9. Neurology is the study of the nervous system, including the brain

10. Dr. Oliver Sacks wrote a book about his patients with neurological disorders

11. One patient actually mistook his wife for a hat

12. Loren Eisley was an anthropologist; he studied human beings and their cultures

13. He wrote such wonderful essays

14. Have you read any of Stephen Jay Gould's books

15. He writes about everything from the physics of baseball to ancient fossils

Revising with Style

Lesson 1 Choosing Effective Details
Answers may vary slightly.

Exercise A

1. Throughout the day in the gravelly desert, a gecko stayed out of the sweltering heat, resting in the shade of a jutting rock.
2. The gecko patiently waited for the sun to set and the air to cool before it foraged for food.
3. When night fell, the hungry gecko darted from under the rock.
4. An unsuspecting grasshopper was the gecko's first meal: the gecko saw the grasshopper near a cactus, snatched it, and then swallowed it whole.
5. The gecko didn't stay to savor the bug; it sensed snakes nearby and scurried away.

Exercise B
Paragraphs will vary. A sample follows.

The day was too beautiful to do nothing at all, so Janine and Hilary set out to hear a concert in the park. That morning they had prepared an elaborate picnic dinner—barbecued chicken, vegetable stew, potato salad, and thick watermelon wedges. Then they packed everything up in a wicker basket and left for the park.

Though they carried a blanket and chairs with their basket and they had to transfer from one train to another and from the last train to a shuttle bus, the hassle was worth it. They knew that cellist Jamin Gonzalez, their favorite musician, would be playing with the symphony orchestra that night. They arrived with time to spare and found a shaded spot on which to spread their blanket. They took out some dishes and napkins and waited for the concert.

They were half-way through their meal, chattering gleefully away, when the cellist came out on stage to the applause of the audience. The two friends quieted immediately and listened intently to the soothing cello. They enjoyed the performance so much that they could hardly believe the sun was already setting over some distant poplars when the last encore had been played. They would remember this day, the two agreed, and in high spirits they returned home.

Lesson 2 Saying More with Less
Answers will vary. Sample answers follow.

1. Born in England in 1862, Kingsley spent much of her youth caring for her sickly mother and brother.
2. Her father expected her to take care of them because he traveled a great deal.
3. In the little free time she had, however, she would read stories that explorers had written about their adventures in Africa.
4. After her parents' death, Kingsley decided to change her life.
5. When she was thirty, she made her first trip to West Africa.
6. Although she was uncertain whether she could manage on her own, her trip was a success.
7. Kingsley felt more at home in West Africa than in England.
8. She lived for a year with the Fang tribe, who accepted her because she brought cloth and tobacco to trade for their ivory and rubber.
9. Although she had no formal education, Kingsley made many scientific discoveries during her trips to West Africa.
10. Before returning to England in 1895, she collected many new and rare species of beetle and fish and made careful ethnological studies of tribal culture.
11. Her travels along the Ogowé River and through jungle to the Rembwé River were all the more remarkable since the region had never been mapped.
12. Before her, nobody had climbed the northeast face of Mount Cameroon, an ascent of 13,350 feet.
13. When Kingsley fell through a camouflaged animal trap onto twelve-inch spikes, she handled the crisis bravely.
14. The books she wrote about her travels were immediate bestsellers.
15. More than a century after her first book was published, Kingsley continues to be admired by thousands of readers.

Revising with Style

Lesson 3 Correcting Commonly Misused Terms I
1. passed; past
2. proceeded; preceded
3. *correct*
4. could of; could have
5. than; then
6. all ready; already
7. a; an
8. among; between
9. except; accept
10. *correct*

Lesson 4 Correcting Commonly Misused Terms II
1. *correct*
2. farther; further
3. amount; number
4. different than; different from
5. sets; sits
6. loose; lose
7. rise; raise
8. irregardless; regardless
9. May; Can
10. let; leave

Lesson 5 Using Pronouns Correctly
Possible answers are provided.
1. they
2. they
3. he or she
4. they
5. they

Lesson 6 Using *Only*
Students should indicate with an arrow the correct position of only. *Corrected sentences follow.*
1. Some people think that having the right name is the only path to success.
2. There was a time when only movie stars and con artists changed their names.
3. The model Norma Jean Baker, for example, changed her name to Marilyn Monroe only a short while after signing her first contract with a film studio.
4. Only a few people know that John Wayne was the stage name of Marion Morrison.
5. John Wayne was not the actor's only stage name; he appeared in his first few films as Duke Morrison.
6. Mathilda isn't the only name that means "brave."
7. Only Graham, however, means "from the gray house."
8. In most states, only an application and a birth certificate are needed to change one's name legally.

Lesson 7 Correcting Double Negatives
Answers will vary. Sample answers follow.
1. I know people that can hardly stand the idea of dining on bugs.
2. There isn't anything wrong with eating bugs.
3. In some Latin American countries, people have no objection to eating the eggs of aquatic insects.
4. It couldn't be any simpler than placing mats underwater for the insects to lay their eggs on.
5. Once the eggs are laid, gatherers don't wait to dry the insects' eggs before making the eggs into cakes.
6. In some African countries, the larvae of honeybees are no less popular than their honey.
7. If you're in the tropics, you shouldn't get too fond of any dragonflies; they may be ground into a paste and served to you.
8. *correct*
9. Somebody had once tried a chocolate-covered grasshopper and had barely noticed the grasshopper.
10. Don't say anything against bug dishes until you've tried them.

Lesson 8 Using Active and Passive Voice
Answers will vary. Sample answers follow.
1. All of us experience five senses—sight, hearing, smell, taste, and touch.
2. *correct*
3. Some of them hear shapes.
4. Others taste colors.
5. Different people perceive this quirk of the brain differently.
6. *correct*
7. *Synesthesia,* a combination of the Greek words *syn* (together) and *aisthesis* (sensation), means "sensing together."
8. In people with synesthesia, one sense triggers another.
9. Many creative people have lived with synesthesia.
10. Writer Vladimir Nabokov saw the letters of the alphabet in colors.
11. He perceived the letter *k,* for example, as huckleberry blue.
12. The composer Aleksandr Scriabin associated colors with musical tones.
13. He heard an A-major chord as green.
14. One person perceived flavors as shapes.
15. This person once described a bland chicken as not having "enough points."

16. Another person tasted baked beans at the sound of the word *Francis*.
17. *correct*
18. Scientists have figured it out only in the last few decades, however.
19. A leading researcher concluded that everyone's brain is capable of synesthesia.
20. Even so, only a few people reach conscious awareness of it.

Lesson 9 Varying Sentence Openers

1. Playing together for the first time in years, the members of the band sounded as good as ever.
2. In his mother's studio, Nate paints watercolors.
3. Grinding, growling, whistling, and hiccuping, the tractor pushed against the heavy log.
4. Sails billowing, the yacht headed out to open sea.
5. Well-fed, energetic, and happy, the dog headed outside to play.
6. Angered, the bull charged the matador.
7. The bicycle tire having been punctured, Jasmine had to walk the bicycle home.
8. Wide-eyed, joyful, and proud, her head lifted high, the producer accepted the Oscar for best picture.
9. Swiftly, holding the football firmly in his arms, Leo ran toward the goal line.
10. For more than a month, Polly could run a five-minute mile.

Lesson 10 Splitting Subject and Verb I

1. One tenant, a tenant on the fifth floor, plays the piano every night.
2. The Olympic swimmer, with every stroke and every kick, was closing in on a world record.
3. Her grandmother's pie, baked entirely from scratch, tasted better than she remembered.
4. The basketball fans, loud and lively, packed into the arena to cheer on their team.
5. A group of Hollywood actors, meeting in secret, formed the Screen Actors Guild in 1933.
6. Smallpox, a deadly virus, was virtually eradicated through vaccinations.
7. The broken water main, in less than ten minutes, had flooded the entire street.
8. Itzhak Perlman, paralyzed in his legs since the age of four, is considered to be one of the world's premier violinists.
9. John Logie Baird, a pioneer in television technology, was the first person to televise moving objects.

10. The detective, having rummaged the crime scene for clues, was still perplexed.

Lesson 11 Splitting Subject and Verb II

Exercise A
1. was
2. *correct*
3. was
4. repaint
5. keeps

Exercise B
Answers may vary. Sample answers follow.
1. The bridge's two main towers, made of structural steel, rise 746 feet above water.
2. New lamps, installed after the fiftieth anniversary of the bridge, make the towers appear taller at night.
3. The bridge's main span, the distance between its two main towers, measures 4,200 feet.
4. This span, for almost thirty years, was the longest in the world.
5. The Akashi-Kaikyo Bridge in Japan, with a main span of 6,532 feet, is now the world's longest suspension bridge.

Lesson 12 Varying Sentence Closers

Exercise A
1. We drove over a hundred miles to the cabin, our home for the summer.
2. My uncle laughed at his own jokes, ruining the punch lines.
3. Celia took charge of the situation, decisively but not offensively.
4. The window washers' scaffold hung near the top of the skyscraper, steadied by nothing more than a few guy wires.
5. Dad came inside from the bitter cold, with icicles hanging from his moustache and eyebrows.

Exercise B
Answers may vary. Sample answers follow.
1. The defendant stared nervously at the jurors, anxious to know their verdict.
2. The Great Balanzini held his arms out and stepped confidently onto the tightrope, a blindfold wrapped snuggly around his head.
3. The creek floods each May, a worrisome month for nearby homeowners.
4. She examined each egg, checking for cracks.

5. Huge cranes moved all about the construction site, hauling girders and stacks of bricks.
6. I can't stop thinking about that movie, romantic yet hilarious.
7. The waiter hurried to our table, our pizza held high above his head.
8. The stream winds for miles through the woods, ending suddenly in a two-hundred-foot waterfall.

Lesson 13 Adding Clauses

1. Jackie Robinson, who joined the Brooklyn Dodgers in 1947, became the first African American to play major-league baseball.
2. Ernest Hemingway, who was rejected for military service several times, entered World War I as an ambulance driver for the Red Cross.
3. Since 1991 the number of books sold each year has risen, even though the number of hours spent surfing the Web has also risen.
4. Fernando speaks Portuguese, which is spoken in both Portugal and Brazil, with the distinctive accent of a Brazilian.
5. Needless to say, when you jog, you should wear supportive shoes.
6. New traffic control systems, which use automated photo technology, may help to discourage drivers from running red lights.

Lesson 14 Inverting Sentence Order I

1. Down came the streamers; down came the signs.
2. Only with an officially stamped ticket could one get in.
3. At the edge of the clearing grew a tiny hosta plant.
4. Happy are the children in the yard next door.
5. Onstage, in front of the curtain, stood the opera stars, smiling and bowing deeply before the crowd.
6. When she made fun of him, was she expecting him to laugh?
7. At the city park was a small bronze statue that Maria recalled having studied one evening to inspire her own art.
8. Not yet settling into our comfortable little house was the new puppy.
9. Isn't this the best peach she has ever tasted?
10. Alongside her stood her two grandparents and her four-year-old brother.
11. On went the lights in every room of the house.
12. Steep and slippery was the path to the base camp, where one could find a cot and a warm meal.

Lesson 15 Inverting Sentence Order II

1. is
2. are
3. C
4. are
5. are
6. do
7. C
8. are
9. lurks
10. does

Lesson 16 Revising for Parallelism I

Answers may vary. Sample answers follow.

1. There are many types of plays, including drama, tragedy, and comedy.
2. Plays may be presented in theaters, open-air spaces, empty stores, or school auditoriums.
3. A play should be an exciting, entertaining, and meaningful experience for the audience.
4. Reading a script is easy, but making a script into a production is challenging.
5. Even a play having only one act and two characters requires much cooperative effort.
6. A director's work consists of analyzing the play, casting roles, working with technicians, and supervising the entire production.
7. Actors must understand their roles, determine their characters' feelings and motivations, and decide how to move and speak.
8. Besides actors, the artists include a scenic designer, lighting designer, and costume designer.
9. The lighting designer arranges multicolored lights to illuminate a scene and support its mood.
10. When various productions of the same play are compared, one may notice vast differences in lighting, in scenery, and in sound effects.

Lesson 17 Revising for Parallelism II

Answers may vary. Sample answers follow.

1. Audiences won't enjoy a play that is boring, long, or confusing.
2. A successful director can not only recognize a good script but also bring that script to life.
3. Actors are, of course, critical to a play's effectiveness and success.
4. Good actors take care both in speaking their lines well and in using even the smallest gestures.
5. A makeup artist can change an actor's appearance through the application of color and shadows or the use of devices such as beards, scars, and wigs.
6. *Correct*
7. A costume designer researches the time period in which the drama is set, designs costumes for the actors that are true to the period, and supervises the manufacture of the clothing.

8. The designer's work must both reflect and support the action, time period, mood, and theme of the play.
9. Drama critics should be people who are familiar with many types of plays and who have a well-developed artistic taste.
10. Drama critics must not only form their own opinions about a play but also be mindful of the message that the director, cast, and designers are trying to convey.

Lesson 18 Combining Sentences I
Answers may vary slightly.

1. The oldest known paintings were created more than thirty thousand years ago yet have survived undamaged.
2. People living many millennia ago carved objects, painted images, and built shelters.
3. Some animals in cave art have grotesquely exaggerated horns.
4. To study prehistoric cultures, anthropologists use several clues: art, fossils, and pollens.
5. The best-known prehistoric cave paintings were discovered more than fifty years ago at Lascaux, France.
6. Other cave paintings have been found at Altamira, Spain; at Vallon-Pont-d'Arc, France; and at Pêche-Merle, France.
7. The artists often worked far at the back of tiny, dimly lit cave chambers.
8. Small stone lamps have been found in some caves.
9. Michel Lorblanchet, a cave archaeologist, is a talented artist.
10. Lorblanchet has figured out prehistoric artists' techniques, re-created their actual experience, and reproduced the Pêche-Merle paintings of horses.

Lesson 19 Combining Sentences II

1. Gargoyles not only funnel rainwater away from the building but also watch over passersby.
2. This gargoyle is carved to look like a lion's head.
3. Gargoyles must have been popular during the rise of Gothic architecture, for they can be seen on many large buildings over 500 years old.
4. Most people think of gargoyles as creatures from medieval cathedrals; still, they are popular to this day.
5. Modern stone carvers have not only captured the old gargoyle styles but also added some contemporary designs.

6. Stone carvers worked on the National Cathedral in Washington, D.C., for more than forty years, yet they carved only 112 gargoyles.
7. Visitors to the National Cathedral can see Darth Vader's menacing face.
8. They can also see a stone lawyer, complete with briefcase, and a gargoyle in a gas mask, so they know they're not looking at a medieval building.

Lesson 20 Combining Sentences III
Answers may vary. Sample answers follow.

1. Leonardo was born in a village called Vinci in 1452.
2. He had a talent for painting colorful, expressive pictures.
3. Apprenticed to the artist Verrocchio after moving to Florence at the age of twelve or thirteen, Leonardo developed his talent.
4. He set up his own shop after close to twelve years of apprenticeship.
5. He then made a decision to move to Milan to work for the duke Lodovico Sforza.
6. Admiring Leonardo's talent, Sforza gave Leonardo a commission to paint *The Last Supper.*
7. Leonardo's *Mona Lisa,* painted after his return to Florence years later, quickly became famous for the subject's mysterious expression.
8. Leonardo used the painting technique of contrasting light and shadow called *chiaroscuro.*
9. He also covered his paintings with tinted varnish to give them a hazy look known as *sfumato.*
10. Until his death in 1519, Leonardo pursued studies in many other fields, including mathematics, botany, and architecture.

Lesson 21 Combining Sentences IV
Answers will vary. Sample answers follow.

1. Ever since Minnie Evans was a child, she had strange waking dreams.
2. Her dreams, which she called "day visions," were filled with fanciful creatures, intricate flowers, and mysterious faces.
3. Minnie's grandmother, whom Minnie called Mama Mary, told her stories about their ancestors in Africa that inspired her childhood drawings.
4. What persuaded her to stop drawing was the ridicule of her friends and the scorn of her teachers.
5. Minnie did not draw again for many years, during which she married, raised three sons, and worked as a housekeeper.

6. When she was forty-three years old, she couldn't ignore the vivid pictures in her head anymore.
7. She began to hang her paintings on the wall of the gatehouse at Airlie Gardens, where she worked as a collector of admission fees.
8. Before Minnie died at the age of ninety-five, she had become a well-known and respected folk artist who never lost sight of her dreams.

Lesson 22 Using Transitions

Answers will vary. Sample answers follow.

1. Rebecca and I count down the days until our vacations just as children count down the days until summer.
2. I go backpacking in remote places, but Rebecca goes sunbathing where there are lots of people.
3. I like to go backpacking because it's inexpensive.
4. I like backpacking because it's affordable. In addition, it's fun.
5. I hiked along the crest of the Appalachian Mountains. I could see miles of forest below.
6. When I came back from all that hiking, I was in the best shape of my life.
7. Improving my physical condition was only a minor benefit. More important, I felt I'd accomplished something.
8. While I was working up a sweat hiking, Rebecca was lying on a beach all day.
9. Since she works as a personal trainer, she wants to take it easy for her vacation.
10. Rebecca is on her feet all day at work. I, on the other hand, sit at a desk.

Lesson 23 Building Coherent Paragraphs I

Paragraph 1

2 First, wash both the melon and the knife you'll be cutting with.

5 With a fork, scrape the seeds from the strips and from the flesh left on the rinds.

3 Then cut the melon in half lengthwise and again in quarters.

1 To de-seed a honeydew melon with a minimum of fuss, follow these few simple steps.

4 Along the seed line of each quarter, cut off a strip of melon flesh and separate the strip from the rest of the melon.

Paragraph 2

4 While the sugar mixture is cooling, purée 5 pounds of melon, seeded and cut into 1-inch cubes, and put the purée in a large bowl.

6 Finally, freeze the whisked mixture in the bowl and scoop out to serve.

1 To make melon ice, first combine 3/4 cup of water and 1 cup of sugar in a medium saucepan and cook over high heat until the mixture boils.

5 Next, pour the cooled sugar mixture into the melon purée, add 2 tablespoons of lime juice, and whisk thoroughly.

2 Reduce the heat by half and stir until the sugar dissolves.

3 When the sugar is entirely dissolved, remove the saucepan from the heat.

Lesson 24 Building Coherent Paragraphs II

Paragraph 1

2 Because having an unpaired electron is unstable, a free radical either takes an electron from or gives an electron to a molecule in a nearby cell of the body.

4 As a result of the deterioration, a person's body becomes aged and diseased.

1 Free radicals, molecules that have one unpaired electron, regularly roam through a person's body.

3 The cells deteriorate in turn from this disruption of their molecules.

Paragraph 2

3 Once in your blood or lymph system, the antioxidants render harmful free radicals in your body harmless.

1 To ward off age and disease, eat foods high in antioxidants, such as broccoli and carrots.

5 Moreover, because the cells are functioning properly, your body won't degenerate as quickly and you just might live longer.

2 By eating these foods, you allow the antioxidants to enter your bloodstream or lymph system through your intestines.

4 Since a smaller number of free radicals is left to attack your body's cells, the cells can continue to function properly.

Lesson 25 Building Coherent Paragraphs III

Paragraph 1
The sentences should be numbered as follows: 2, 6, 3, 1, 5, 4.

Paragraph 2
The sentences should be numbered as follows: 3, 1, 6, 5, 2, 4.

Lesson 26 Building Coherent Paragraphs IV
Answers will vary. A sample answer follows.

By subject

 Although the two largest cities in the United States, New York and Los Angeles, share some qualities due to their massive size, they are also different in many ways. New York, the country's largest city, is a financial and cultural capital with international influence. People from around the world gather there to take advantage of its opportunities, and the diversity makes the city a vibrant place. With almost eight million people living in an area of 304 square miles, the population is extremely dense. People usually walk, taxi, or take public transportation from place to place. New York has a temperate climate with four distinct seasons, but the presence of snow in the winter does not keep pedestrians off the street. Los Angeles is the United States' second largest city. Like New York, it is a financial and cultural capital whose impact is felt around the world. Also like New York, the world's citizens come to the city's doors: its multicultural population adds to its character. However, the citizens of Los Angeles have more room to spread out than New Yorkers do. The three and a half million people in the West Coast city inhabit an area of 464 square miles. Another difference between New York and Los Angeles is that Los Angelenos tend to use private cars as their primary mode of transportation. They are less likely to take a subway, a taxi, or a bus than New Yorkers are. Furthermore, the people of Los Angeles enjoy a climate that does not change drastically throughout the year. The city lies in a semitropical zone, so while palm trees are a frequent site, snowflakes are not.

Lesson 27 Creating Unity in Paragraphs

Exercise A
The following sentences should be marked for deletion.
1. Which time of day are you more alert?
2. The people of Peru speak Spanish.
3. Their fireplaces were very cozy.

4. They didn't have a Pony Express.
5. Slavery is a moral outrage.

Exercise B
A paragraph symbol should be inserted at the start of the seventh sentence (beginning "The Internet has other problems") and the thirteenth sentence (beginning "However, for most teens").

Lesson 28 Understanding Elaboration
Answers may vary. Sample answers follow.
1. Statistics; students may underline the second and third sentence.
2. Example, facts; students may underline the second and third sentence.
3. Example; students may underline the second sentence.
4. Descriptive details, anecdote; students may underline "the one in the modernistic building of concrete and glass that we visited the same day," and the second sentence.
5. Examples; students may underline "MTV has also aired public service programs about political, social, and environmental issues" and "winning a prestigious Peabody Award."

Lesson 29 Elaborating to Persuade
Answers will vary. Sample answers follow.
1. Town developers should use the site vacated by the old factory to create a municipal park, not a new mall. After all, we already have places where we can buy clothes and electronics, see movies, and dine comfortably, but we don't have a good place for the simple pleasures of picnicking, walking dogs, playing softball or tennis, or running around on a wide expanse of green grass. Moreover, building another mall would produce additional traffic and smog in an already congested and polluted area. The kinds of trees that would be planted in a new park, however, would help reduce the amount of air pollution we already have.
2. Students who wish to go to the prom only to dance should not be forced to buy tickets to the dinner beforehand. I realize that prom organizers are hoping to ensure a big turnout, but their policy is more likely to ensure the opposite. Some students, for instance, may not have enough money for both the dinner and the dance and will have to decline to go altogether. Students who do have the money may wish to dine privately with their dates. This second group of students are

Revising with Style

unlikely to enjoy the dinner and could dampen the high spirits of those who would enjoy it. Or, as with the first group of students, they may simply not bother to go.

3. The school year has become too long; our principal should shorten it. There are two types of student who would truly benefit from the change. The first is the one who goes, willingly or not, to summer school. As things stand, that student has only two weeks to relax before the fall term begins and may be in danger of being too exhausted to do well in fall classes. The second is the one whose summer extracurricular activities—whether music camp, athletic camp, an internship, or study abroad—overlaps with the first week or so of the school year. Students of this type must either miss a few days of class and fall behind or be prevented from developing talents they might never have realized they had.

4. If a desired course is not offered at our school, qualified students should be allowed to take it at a local community college instead. Ours is a good school, but there are a few areas in which it is deficient. One area is math. Students who are ahead by a grade or more in math cannot continue to excel once they reach junior or senior year. By taking classes at a local college, they'd not only deepen their knowledge in math but also become familiar with college life.

5. Parents and teachers are debating whether to open the school library during after-school hours. Though keeping it open will surely cost money, it's worth the expense. I can recall several papers I turned in that would have been much improved if I had been able to stay later at the school library. I tried using my study period for research, but a single period barely gave me enough time to look up a book, locate it on the shelf, and find a place to work. In addition, students who lack their own private study space at home or who have noisy siblings could do their homework in the library before heading home from school.

Lesson 30 Finding Your Voice

Exercise A
1. B
2. A
3. A
4. C
5. B

Exercise B
Answers will vary. Sample answers follow.

1. The year 1998 was an exciting one for baseball. Mark McGwire, the Herculean first baseman for the St. Louis Cardinals, hit a whopping seventy home runs in one season. Nobody had come near the record for over thirty years until Mac just smashed it by hitting nine more dingers than the Yankees' Roger Maris did.

2. If Congress is so concerned about how well teenagers do in school, why doesn't it pass a law to raise the minimum wage? Those of us who work after school don't just buy the latest CDs or go to movies with what we earn. We also buy books or save for college. More important, by getting paid more, we could work fewer hours. The less time we work, the more time we'll have to study for exams or practice our music or do whatever else will make us better, more educated people.

Lesson 31 Identifying Metaphors, Similes, and Personification

Exercise A
1. simile
2. metaphor
3. personification
4. simile
5. metaphor
6. personification
7. simile
8. simile
9. personification
10. metaphor

Exercise B
Answers will vary. Sample answers follow.

1. The airplane spiraled overhead like a hungry vulture zeroing in on a meal.
2. White sheets billowed on the clothesline like sails on a clipper ship.
3. The water of the lake was as clear as a just-cleaned window.
4. When the immigrants were sworn in as citizens, Lady Liberty watched the ceremony proudly.
5. The road silently snakes through the forest.
6. Playing the guitar is my passport to other cultures.
7. The skateboarders twirled in midair like high-wire acrobats.
8. An army of ants invaded our kitchen.

Revising with Style

Lesson 32 Identifying Hyperbole and Understatement

Exercise A
1. understatement
2. understatement
3. hyperbole
4. understatement
5. hyperbole
6. understatement
7. hyperbole
8. hyperbole
9. hyperbole
10. understatement

Exercise B
Answers will vary. Sample answers follow.
1. I love playing basketball more than anything else in the world.
2. Dave's sand castle put Buckingham Palace to shame.
3. Dennis was mildly pleased when the Steelers won the Super Bowl.
4. The Marquez family seems richer than Bill Gates, Ted Turner, and the Queen of England combined.
5. Jessica may be a wee bit tired; she fell asleep at the lunch table today.
6. When Amy wore her alligator shoes, she attracted about as much attention as an alligator walking down Main Street in a sundress and sneakers.
7. I hate cleaning house more than I would hate being pecked to death by ducks.
8. Video games consume so much time that I can hardly eat, sleep, or brush my teeth.
9. People who talk on the phone while they drive have no idea whether the car in front of them is stopping, turning, or taking off into full flight.
10. Mark was so disappointed about getting a D on the test that he hasn't taken his nose out of the textbook since.
11. Lilacs smell sweeter than the nectar of the gods.
12. Stephen has a few books.

Lesson 33 Identifying Errors in Logic
1. false cause
2. loaded language
3. stereotyping
4. false analogy
5. limited sample
6. false cause
7. false analogy
8. limited sample
9. loaded language
10. stereotyping

Lesson 34 Avoiding Clichés and Sexist Language

Exercise A
1. worth his salt; sexist
2. tugging at readers' heartstrings; sexist
3. not for the faint of heart
4. true blue, a snake in the grass
5. green thumb; sexist

Exercise B
Answers will vary. Sample answers follow.
1. Every engineer at the conference brought visual aids.
2. Firefighters risk their lives every day putting out fires.
3. On our flight to San Francisco, the flight attendants were very helpful.
4. My cousin Chris could lift the back of a pickup truck without straining.
5. Every athlete at the Olympics represents his or her country with pride.
6. Registered nurses make use of their training with every patient they see.
7. Abel passed his driving exam easily.
8. The server apologized for mixing up our orders.
9. Research scientists choose their career paths based on their interests.
10. When Jamal bumped his head on that pipe, he nearly fainted.

Lesson 35 Proofreading I
1. **O**ne of my favorite **f**antasy writers is **E**sther **F**riesner.
2. **F**riesner was born in **N**ew **Y**ork **C**ity in 1951.
3. Her parents both taught in the **B**rooklyn school system; her **m**other taught English and her **f**ather taught **S**panish, **L**atin, **I**talian, and algebra.
4. "I liked to **w**rite at an early age," said Friesner. "In fact, I started making stories when **I** was three."
5. **T**he first writing she ever sold was an article for *Cats* magazine.
6. Many of her early **s**tories were rejected by Isaac **A**simov's **m**agazine.
7. Friesner kept trying and has now published more than twenty **n**ovels, starting with *Mustapha and His Wise Dog*.
8. Reviewer **F**red **L**erner wrote in *Voice of Youth Advocates* that Friesner is "**o**ne of the funniest" writers of fantasy fiction.

Lesson 36 Proofreading II

Exercise A
1. Many people consider Edgar Allan **Poe's** short story "The **Murders** in the Rue Morgue," published in 1841, the first detective story.
2. *C*
3. Arthur Conan **Doyle's** Sherlock Holmes was another famous literary detective.

90

Revising with Style

4. **Holmes's** specialty was to solve every crime by detailed reasoning, and he always minded his **p's** and **q's.**

5. In the 1900s, Mary Roberts **Rinehart's** and G. K. **Chesterton's** writing careers began.

6. The **'20s** saw Agatha Christie's first novels, featuring Hercule **Poirot's** sleuthing, which **couldn't** have been more entertaining to **readers.**

7. Do you prefer Raymond **Chandler's** journeys down the mean **streets** of Los Angeles to Joyce Carol **Oates's** psychological studies?

8. *C*

9. Nevada **Barr's** career as a national park ranger **wasn't** wasted when she began a mystery series **whose** hero, Anna Pigeon, is a park ranger.

10. Especially popular today are detectives who understand the inner workings of **men's** and **women's** minds.

Exercise B

1. Did you hear Keisha say, "**I'm** hosting a party at my **aunt's** house"?

2. Leonardo and **Fidel's** father owns an electronics repair shop.

3. **Arthur's** and **Lisa's** math classes are using the same textbook.

4. **Everyone's** participation is needed to guarantee the success of the **school's** drive for **coats** and shoes for the homeless.

5. **We're** constantly reminded of the old adage "You **can't** judge a book by **its** cover."

6. All the family enjoyed listening to **Great-Grandfather's** stories about the blizzard of **'88**—that's 1888, of course.

7. The business **partners** were aware that they needed a formal contract, not merely a "**gentleman's** agreement."

8. The campers couldn't believe that they were lost in spite of following their **leader's** directions to the campsite and her advice to bring a compass.

9. The **twins'** summer jobs in their **brother-in-law's** store left them little time to enjoy water sports at their **parents'** cottage.

10. The **students'** objections to the **school's** uniform policy **doesn't** give them the right to ignore it.

Lesson 37 Proofreading III

Exercise A

1. More often than **ideals,** economics fuel revolutions.

2. In **France,** for **example,** extreme poverty resulted in the French **Revolution,** a conflict between economic and social classes.

3. As for the American **Revolution,** it stemmed partly from taxation without representation.

4. Early in the **conflict,** angry **colonists,** disguised as Native Americans and wielding **hatchets,** boarded British ships and tossed their cargo of tea into Boston Harbor.

5. Many **colonists who** owned or could obtain a **weapon helped** fight the British.

6. The British **troops,** who were reputed to be a fine fighting **force,** made easy targets for the muskets of the ragtag colonial militia.

7. While the colonists **fought,** their wives maintained their farms and businesses.

8. Valley **Forge,** where Washington's troops **wintered during** the American **Revolution,** is located in Pennsylvania.

9. The early patriots had **wisdom, courage,** and determination.

10. Having sacrificed to make a better life in the New **World,** they would not surrender to the demands of Great Britain.

11. After winning the Revolutionary **War,** the colonists faced the difficult tasks of forming a new government and developing an unfamiliar country.

12. The pioneers who settled the West struggled to build **homes,** to cultivate the **land,** and to defend themselves against hostile forces.

13. When American farmers pushed **westward,** they caused resentment in those who owned ranches or herded cattle for a living.

14. The Mexican **War,** begun in **1846,** was an attempt to settle a border dispute.

15. One of the battle **sites was** the **Alamo,** a venerable old Spanish mission.

Exercise B

1. Because the weather was atypically **cold,** few people could enjoy summer **sports,** such as **swimming, boating,** and picnicking.

2. On the Fourth of **July, however,** everyone in our family had a marvelous time.

3. We made a festive picnic **lunch,** which we **ate in** the den.

4. A softball game involving **children, teenagers,** and **adults provided** fun and exercise in the afternoon.

5. As soon as dusk **fell,** we got ready to watch the fireworks **and, oh,** were they spectacular!

6. In my **opinion,** the fireworks **display,** as beautiful as it **was,** could have been longer.

7. **Although we** had enjoyed **ourselves,** we were not ready to end the day's activities.

8. Putting on sweaters and light **jackets,** we walked to the ice cream **shop,** where we bought our favorite desserts.

9. With our hands full of good **things to eat,** we hurried back home.

10. Huddling together in the **den,** we watched a **scary,** exciting movie.

Lesson 38 Proofreading IV

Exercise A

1. The school library has a wide selection of books by modern American **authors,** doesn't it?

2. The neighborhood library moved to its new site on September **1,** 1999.

3. **Lorraine,** have you ever visited the city's central library?

4. The librarian gave me the address of the House of Representatives in **Washington,** D.C.

5. Will you be in Washington when Congress is in **session, Melanie,** or will you be there during the annual recess?

Exercise B

2054 Sunset Place
Brookhaven, MN 56587
August **5,** 2001

Dear Ruth **Ellen,**

I'm sorry I haven't **written,** but I'm answering your letter now before you become Ruth Ellen **Carson,** M.D. As you might have guessed, I've been really busy. For my social studies **class,** our group is polling voters in the school elections. That **is,** we're asking people ahead of time whom they're planning to vote for. We've chosen a representative sample of **students,** and every **week,** we check in with them. This project uses our people **skills,** our math **skills,** and our computer skills. You can imagine how time-consuming it **is,** can't you?

Taking up the rest of my **time is reading,** which I still love. I've been especially interested in **biographies and** autobiographies. Among my

favorites are books by Jill Ker **Conway,** Jean **Fritz,** and Russell Baker. Daniel Pinkwater has a fascinating, **insightful,** hilarious memoir called *Chicago Days/Hoboken Nights*. He's a **writer who** always makes me laugh.

I'm sending you a review about an anthology of essays called *The Autobiographical Eye*. I haven't found the book **yet,** but the review appeared on page **3 of** the *Donegal Bulletin* on April **7,** 2000. I remember that fiction is your first **love,** so perhaps you will enjoy reading about the **lives, loves,** and inspirations of some of your favorite fiction writers.

Sincerely,

Jared

Lesson 39 Proofreading V

Sentences 4, 11, and 13 may end with either an exclamation point or a period.

1. Have you heard of Rachel **Carson?**

2. She has been called the mother of the environmental **movement.**

3. This biologist was one of the first people to see that we were poisoning our **environment.**

4. The warnings in her book *Silent Spring* are so **frightening!**

5. Don't you agree that physics is another interesting scientific **field?**

6. Researchers in this field study the behavior of galaxies as well as particles smaller than **atoms.**

7. Who doesn't have a desire to understand the way the universe **works?**

8. In his book *The Elegant Universe,* physicist Brian Greene asks questions about how the universe began and whether time travel is **possible.**

9. Neurology is the study of the nervous system, including the **brain.**

10. Dr. Oliver Sacks wrote a book about his patients with neurological **disorders.**

11. One patient actually mistook his wife for a **hat!**

12. Loren Eisley was an anthropologist; he studied human beings and their **cultures.**

13. He wrote such wonderful **essays!**

14. Have you read any of Stephen Jay Gould's **books?**

15. He writes about everything from the physics of baseball to ancient **fossils.**